Apocalyptic: Ancient and Modern

D. S. RUSSELL

Apocalyptic:

Ancient and Modern

SCM PRESS LTD

334 00044 0
First published 1978
by SCM Press Ltd
58 Bloomsbury Street London WC1

Filmset in 'Monophoto' Ehrhardt 11 on 12½ pt. by
Richard Clay (The Chaucer Press), Ltd., Bungay, Suffolk
and printed in Great Britain by
Fletcher & Son Ltd., Norwich

CONTENTS

IV TODAY AND TOMORROW

PREFACE

Some years have passed since I last put pen to paper in an attempt to unravel some of the 'mysteries' of the Jewish apocalyptic writers of the inter-testamental period. At that time I was helped by the discipline of the lecture room and senior common room and the give and take of academic debate.

In more recent years the university and college classrooms have given way to the hurly-burly of church administration and inter-church relations. My forays into the academic world have taken the form of occasional lectures and sporadic attempts to keep in touch with a never-ceasing flow of books.

But all has not been loss. World travel, care of the churches, inter-church debate, involvement in human rights – all these have helped, in however limited a way, to broaden the mind and, hopefully, to deepen the understanding.

It was against this background and in this setting that these four lectures were prepared. They are an attempt to see more clearly the message which the early Jewish apocalyptic writers had for the days in which they lived and, again hopefully, something of its meaning for us today. The subject is 'Apocalyptic, ancient and modern'. The treatment in the event may be more ancient and less modern, but I hope I have conveyed my conviction that these writers, for all their strange and bizarre ideas, still have something worth while to say to our modern generation.

The occasion which led to the preparation of the first three of the lectures was an invitation to deliver the Nordenhaug

Memorial Lectures in the Baptist Seminary in Ruschlikon, Switzerland. Dr Joseph Nordenhaug served as President of the Seminary and subsequently became General Secretary of the Baptist World Alliance. He was an outstanding Christian leader, combining in his person the many different gifts of scholar, teacher, preacher, communicator and administrator.

A subsequent invitation to deliver the Hayward Lectures, established by the late Mrs C. C. Hayward, at Acadia University, Nova Scotia, under the auspices of the Acadia Divinity College, provided the incentive to revise these three lectures and to add a fourth.

I am deeply grateful to the President and staff of Ruschlikon Seminary and to the Principal and staff of Acadia Divinity College for the sincerity of their welcome and the warmth of their hospitality.

I also acknowledge my deep indebtedness to Miss Marjorie Wass for her patience and industry in deciphering the hiero-glyphics of my handwriting and in typing and retyping the manuscript amid her many other secretarial responsibilities.

Baptist Church House
London
December 1977

The Hayward Lectures
and
The Nordenhaug Memorial
Lectures

Dedicated to
Georgina and Michael
Two Grand Children

I

An Age of Crisis

1 *The apocalyptic books*

Away back in 1943 I was first introduced to the Jewish apocalyptic writings of the inter-testamental period by my old college principal, H. Wheeler Robinson. I found myself in a weird and wonderful world of fantasy and dreams – beasts with sprouting horns, dragons spouting fire, falling stars, mysterious horsemen, mystical mountains, sacred rivers, devastating earthquakes, fearsome giants, demon progeny, monstrous births, portents in heaven, portents on earth. Its often frenzied and frenetic descriptions of coming woes sounded like the product of over-heated minds.

After a while my feeling of bemusement began to change to one of appreciation, first of the literary form of apocalyptic and then of its message. Its literary form, of course, is that of poetry of a vivid and highly imaginative kind. To treat it as if it were cold prose, to be dissected and analysed and assessed, is to end up with a dead misshapen thing unworthy of the name of literature, far less of revelation. To appreciate its message, it is necessary to enter into the mind and mood of the writer, to gauge the depths of his feelings and to understand the medium he uses to express his deeply felt convictions. The fact that that medium is a form of writing which is stilted, exaggerated and often grotesque, should not blind us to the content of the message he is trying to convey. To demythologize is difficult at the best of times. To do so with apocalyptic is to attempt the impossible. Content and form belong together; message and myth are of the same stuff. To separate them is to bid farewell to a dream; and apocalyptic is made up of dreams. Sometimes they are visions; sometimes hallucinations. The one must be taken with the other, the good with the bad, the gold with the dross.

But what are we to make of its message? What indeed! Shortly after I had been introduced to this literature there was published, in 1944, a slim volume, later revised and enlarged, which helped me greatly. I refer to H. H. Rowley's *The Relevance of Apocalyptic*.[1] In brief compass the writer lucidly describes the rise of this peculiar style of writing among the Jews of Palestine and the Dispersion in the second century BC and then goes on to list and analyse the many apocalyptic writings produced at that time, from the book of Daniel in the reign of Antiochus Epiphanes in 165 BC through to the book of Revelation at the turn of the first century AD. In the later edition of Dr Rowley's book this list is augmented by reference to the Dead Sea Scrolls some of which are apocalyptic in character and cast further light on the significant role played by this type of literature in the religious and political thinking of the inter-testamental period.

The very title of the book indicates clearly the apologetic purpose he has in writing. It is to demonstrate the 'relevance' of apocalyptic for succeeding generations and to spell out what he calls its 'enduring message'. A successor of his in the chair of Semitic Languages and Literatures in the University of Manchester, James Barr, has criticized this method and in particular Rowley's use of his material as doctrine and his endeavour to extract from apocalyptic 'those elements which had abiding value ... in a situation that is basically non-apocalyptic in its attitudes and sympathies'.[2] I take the point that the apocalyptic writers did not set themselves to write doctrinal treatises, nor should their works be read as such and their 'truths' applied out of context in totally different historical situations. Nevertheless, I would defend Dr Rowley's use of the word 'relevance' in the title of his book to this extent that our own generation is in so many ways strikingly like that in which the apocalyptic message was first given. I venture to think that in these none-too-dissimilar 'apocalyptic' days the message of ancient apocalyptic is not altogether *irrelevant*.

But what was this ancient apocalyptic and how did it arise? Well, essentially it was a literary phenomenon that emerged in Judaism during the reign of the Seleucid king, Antiochus Epiphanes (175–163 BC). The word 'apocalyptic' is derived from the Greek noun *apokalypsis*, meaning 'revelation'. Its use, however, with reference to this *genre* of literature is due in all probability not to the revelatory character of the books in question but rather to the fact that they have much in common with the New Testament Apocalypse with its esoteric language, its bizarre imagery and its pronouncements concerning the consummation of all things in fulfilment of the promises of God.

Their 'setting in life' is difficult to identify, but it would appear that, even though their actual composition may have belonged to certain restricted circles of 'the wise' within Judaism, in course of time their teaching made a popular appeal to the Jewish people as a whole. It would be wrong to confine their production or their use to any one party within Judaism. Be that as it may, there is good reason to believe that right through the oppressive reigns of the Herodian kings and the testing years of the Roman procurators, culminating in the Jewish War of AD 66, they were a considerable source of encouragement and strength to the entire Jewish people as they faced dire peril and the threat of extinction at the hands of their enemies. They demonstrated how moral and spiritual resistance can challenge despots and tyrants and even lay them low.

In course of time Christians began to produce their own apocalyptic literature which is hardly to be distinguished in its style and presentation from the Jewish literature that had gone before. There are the same emphases and the same imagery. The chief, and indeed cardinal, difference between them is to

3

be found in the person of Jesus Christ who is here given the place of pre-eminence and in whom the hopes of God's people are at last fulfilled. This is exemplified most clearly in the book of Revelation, the greatest of all Christian apocalyptic writings. Many of the Jewish apocalyptic *motifs* are to be found here, so much so that some scholars have identified its nucleus as a Jewish writing. As in the case of Jewish apocalyptic, this book also appears in a time of crisis and dire persecution for the people of God.

2 *The rediscovery of apocalyptic*

For many years, it can be said, apocalyptic has tended to be the Cinderella among biblical and theological studies and its relevance for our understanding of the Jewish tradition and the Christian message alike has been called in question. More recently, however, there has been a revival of interest, not least among biblical and systematic theologians. This is brought out clearly by Klaus Koch in a book with the significant title *The Rediscovery of Apocalyptic*. In the second chapter, entitled, 'The Apocalyptic Renaissance', he outlines the revival, in post-war years, of theological and literary interest in this class of literature among German speaking people in particular. He refers to two seminal writers – Ernst Käsemann and his essay on 'The Beginnings of Christian Theology'[3] published in 1960 and, in the field of systematic theology, to Wolfhart Pannenberg who, in 1959, gave renewed importance to the apocalyptic concept of history for Christian theology in his essay 'Redemptive Event and History'.[4] This renewed interest in apocalyptic within theological circles is evident also in Britain and in the United States of America. It has not, however, been confined to such circles but has shown itself also in the realms of art and literature and in philosophical thinking over the past thirty years or so.[5]

Koch suggests that this 'sudden turning to apocalyptic' has been prompted by a fresh study of the texts and has gained its chief impetus from the questionings of New Testament scholarship or systematic theology. It may be, however, that there is a deeper reason still for this revitalized interest and concern. Apocalyptic, like any other style of writing or religious thought, has to be understood within its historical framework, and it is not without significance that the period within which Jewish apocalyptic grew and flourished was at one and the same time one of the most heroic and one of the most tragic in Israel's history. It was an era of severe testing – of persecution, suffering and death – when the hearts of the faithful longed passionately for the breaking in of God upon human affairs and the destruction of the wicked. These books reflect in a poignant and dramatic way the response of deeply religious people to the terrible pressures and persecutions of their time. *An apocalyptic age*

For this reason the revival or rediscovery of apocalyptic in theological study during the past generation is perhaps not surprising; for between the two centuries or so preceding the Christian era and the greater part of the twentieth century there is a marked affinity which engenders sympathy and understanding. Each is an age of crisis – politically, socially and religiously – when long established institutions and deeply rooted beliefs have come under severe attack, sometimes from within and at other times from an external source. Belsen and Buchenwald, for the enormity of the crimes committed there, have perhaps no parallel in human history, but the treatment meted out by, say, Antiochus Epiphanes to the Jews of his day had within it the same root of evil. Repression of and discrimination against political and religious minorities today reflect faithfully the experience of both Jews and Christians at times when the religion of each was outlawed as *religio illicita*. This generation's challenge to 'orthodox' faith and the assertion that 'God is dead' remind us of the even more traumatic challenges levelled at the faithful in the days between Alexander the Great and the reign of Tiberius Caesar, with their clash of cultures and their denial of 'the God of our fathers'.

5

Apocalyptic is a language of crisis; in times of stress it lifts up its voice to give needed assurance to God's people. In its Jewish literary expression it must have had a fairly long pre-history in the form of oral tradition and certainly has had a prolonged post-history in both Jewish and Christian circles. Like an underground stream it has flowed on undetected, sometimes for centuries at a time, breaking surface every now and again, particularly in times of crisis and persecution, to bring refreshment and strength to the harassed people of God. The hopes and fears expressed in the apocalyptic writings are always there, just below the surface of religious thought and experience. They may find new expression and renewed interpretation but their essential message has a relevance in every age of crisis, not least our own.

The object of this chapter is to compare the historical situations of then and now and indicate the similarities between them, allowing the one to cast light on the other, letting history as it were speak to history. In chapter II we shall look more closely at the content of the apocalyptic message which grew and grows out of these historical situations and try to assess its value for our understanding of history and event in our modern world. In chapter III we shall examine the place of apocalyptic ideas, and especially the concept of the kingdom of God, in the preached message of the early church, particularly as this is delineated in the synoptic gospels, and comment upon its place in present-day preaching. In chapter IV we shall reflect on hopes and fears for the future expressed by some modern writers who make use at times of apocalyptic language, and try to draw out some theological findings from what they say.

3 *A conflation of cultures*

In comparing the two historical situations in question we are struck by the fact that each is marked by a confusing conflation of cultures. Reference is often made to our present-day world as a 'global village'. Many things separate nation from nation, race from race, culture from culture. But there are significant factors which unite them and make them one. One is the ease and speed of travel; another is a greater openness to our neighbours; another is the threat of war and of atomic extinction; yet another is the intermingling of diverse cultures.

In the years preceding the appearance of the Jewish apocalyptic literature *oikumené* had become a reality through the conquests and policies of Alexander the Great and his successors. It was his avowed purpose to fuse the two civilizations of East and West by means of the Greek culture which he himself had embraced and whose protagonist he set himself to be. The name 'Hellenism' is usually applied to that Greek culture and civilization which characterized 'the inhabited world' from the time of Alexander right through to Roman times. Barriers of all kinds were thrown down – political, national and cultural – and men from totally different backgrounds found themselves swept up into a culture which challenged powerfully their long-established beliefs and institutions.

Reference is made in Josephus, Eusebius and elsewhere to one Berossus, a Chaldean priest of the third century BC, who was representative of a Magian missionary movement which made its way throughout the Eastern Mediterranean 'preaching a Greek-philosophized blend of Iranian esotericism with Chaldean astrology and determinism'.[6] Alexander had already made a significant breach in the cultural barrier between East and West, making possible not only the spread of Greek civilization in the East through the planting of new cities, through trade, through marriage and the like, but also the spread of Oriental civilization whose ideas and influences deeply affected the thinking of Jew and pagan alike. The Persian empire which Alexander now took under his wing had itself absorbed the old Babylonian empire with its teaching concerning astrology, occultism, cosmology and angelology. The religion of Zoroaster, belonging to the old Persian empire, injected its beliefs concerning the determinism of history, the doctrine of the 'two ages', the destruction of the world and the fact of the final judgment. The resulting conglomerate culture was a breeding ground for syncretistic religions and philosophies which made their influence felt within Judaism and conditioned Jewish writers along with others. It is against this background of Jewish–Hellenistic–Oriental syncretism that we are to understand the Jewish apocalyptic writers. Their thought and expression cannot be explained simply in terms of their Hebrew heritage. This diverse culture is the seed-bed from which their visions and revelations grew.

This account of the influence of East upon West and of the resulting conflation of different cultures has a familiar ring about it today in most of the large cities of Western Europe. Saffron robed Buddhist monks are a familiar sight in the streets of London while the practice of Yoga and of transcendental meditation is commonplace among the sophisticated and not-so-sophisticated young. Hindu 'missionaries' based on Hindu temples seek converts among the uncommitted and advocate a syncretism alien to the Jewish and the Christian faiths. The reverse process is also true. Many young people from Western society, educated in the science and religion of the West, have made their way eastwards to live, think and pray at the feet of *gurus* and other holy men. The influence of such intermingling of cultures on the established Christian religion of the West is limited, but there has developed an open-ended society whose influence on Western culture will surely be far-reaching.

Already, in not a few countries in the West, the multicultural, multi-racial and multi-faith society is presenting a challenge and an opportunity to governments, and not least to the Christian church. As yet it has not been accepted seriously enough by the bulk of the people nor, it would seem, has the church as yet identified its role in this difficult situation. The result is at times tension and misunderstanding, leading to bitterness and resentment. A new society is travailing in birth and has not yet been brought forth. It is interesting to note that this very language of travail and birth was used by an apocalyptic writer long ago at Qumran in his description, in one of the Hymns of Thanksgiving, of the coming kingdom.[7] The struggle for such identity still has apocalyptic overtones today.

4 *Pressures to conform*

To the pious Jews Hellenism was a challenge to the Jewish faith not simply because it introduced foreign religions and foreign gods but because it represented a way of life altogether foreign to that of their fathers. What they faced was the challenge not so much of a rival religion as of a rival culture to which they were being forced to conform. It represented a manner or style of life which was *anathema* to them and had to be resisted to the death.

A crucial factor in the spread of this Hellenistic culture was the founding throughout Palestine and the Dispersion of 'Greek' cities, i.e. cities organized and governed on the Greek pattern, whose inhabitants were thoroughly indoctrinated in a mode of living which they speedily made their own. In the realm of politics the democratic senate resembling the Athenian *Boulé* effected a quite new mental outlook, while the gymnasium and the youth centre provided a form of education and recreation which found willing and responsive students. The hippodrome and the athletic stadium, the theatre and the music-hall added their quota. On a more academic plane literature and the arts flourished. The Greek language was 'fashionable'. Greek manners and Greek dress were the mark of sophistication. This was particularly marked among the young who proudly wore the fashionable wide-brimmed hat, the high-laced boots and the loose cloak thrown over the shoulder and fastened on with brooches. The Hellenistic way of life was 'civilized' – so unlike the boorish and frumpish parochialism of their fathers.

9

But there was a much darker side to this 'enlightened' style of living which unsuccessfully concealed a degeneracy and rottenness which contained the seeds of its own destruction. This was seen not only in gluttony and drunkenness, but also in immorality and vice. Athletics were more than a display of prowess and physical fitness. They were an occasion for religious rites and ceremonies to which the competitors had to submit themselves, whether they were pagans or Jews. Some of these were far removed from the monotheism of Judaism and from the ethical purity of the prophets. To be accepted one had to conform. And so we find Jewish athletes making themselves 'uncircumcised' so as to avoid the derision of the crowds. Youths changed their Hebrew names into Greek and fathers saved future embarrassment by giving their children Greek names from birth. Hellenism was all-pervasive and all-demanding.

The apocalyptic writers were among those who, in the time of Antiochus Epiphanes, were to register their protest and rebel against the accursed thing that was intent on killing the faith of their fathers. The party of the Hasidim or Pious Ones was to voice a protest which would be heard throughout the land. It was one of their number, in all probability, who in or around the year 165 BC was to produce the first Jewish apocalyptic writing worthy of that name, the book of Daniel, which reflected the outlook of his party and which was to have such an influence on subsequent writers and religious thinkers. It was a protest against submission to an alien culture; it was an encouragement to remain stedfast and endure to the end; it was a pointer to the fact that that end was near at hand and the kingdom of God would soon be ushered in.

The pressures to conform are powerful factors in many civilizations and not least in our own. They are felt by every member, but in a particular and peculiar way by those who try to maintain a belief in God in the midst of a secular environment or to live a God-directed life in a society which has little or no room for the Judaeo-Christian ethic. Such pressures are felt at every level of social and political life as well as in the schools and in places of employment.

Within an officially *atheistic* society they are particularly powerful and far-reaching in their demands upon the individual, especially when they operate with the full support and sanction of the governing authorities. A person's private morals, his religion, the books he writes, the literature he reads, the scientific theories he propounds – all are influenced deeply by the culture within which he lives. He must conform or else face dire results. Such conformity is often coercive, having behind it political and police power which has as its objective submission to and acceptance of the system and the culture as the only means of achieving the ultimate good. The Jewish and Christian religions have had to come to terms with such pressures, not least in Eastern Europe, and it is of interest to observe the place which the apocalyptic hope has come to hold there in private devotion and in public preaching.

Such pressures, however, are to be found also in countries where there has been a long history of traditional Christianity and where the politics of the ruling authorities are diametrically opposed to those of Eastern Europe. In this connection it is interesting to observe the growth of the so-called 'liberation theology' in the continent of South America, not least under totalitarian regimes, and the 'apocalyptic' note that is struck there again and again. This, as we shall see in chapter II, may be quite different in content and emphasis from that of the inter-testamental period. Nevertheless it portrays the same hopes and fears and is expressed with a like urgency.

Western Europe and the North American continent may not be subjected to such pressures normally associated with the political left and the political right, but those they do endure are no less insidious and severe. Life in the secular city and in secular society is not conducive to true religion and seems to have little in common with the claims of the rule of God over the lives of men and society. The institutions of communism and capitalism alike have to be assessed in terms of the kingdom and, where they fall short, come under the judgment of God. It is not without significance that the word 'crisis' with which the West is so familiar means literally 'judgment', and judgment lies very close to the heart of the apocalyptic message in whatever generation it is preached.

5 *State and church*

The apocalyptists, however, had to confront not just a rival culture but also what the New Testament calls 'principalities and powers in high places'. In their writings they gave a spiritual interpretation to these things, but the opposition they faced, which was the incentive behind their writings, was the plain fact of tyranny and oppression in the shape of king and state. The real trouble began with Antiochus IV, the Seleucid king who in 169 BC adopted the title *Theos Epiphanes* ('God Manifest'), and three years later added to it the epithet *Nicephorus* ('Victorious'). On some of the coins dating from his reign there appears the face of Zeus with features that bear a close resemblance to Antiochus himself, and there are indications that he encouraged his subjects to worship him as divine. There was, of course, nothing very new about this. Alexander the Great and other Seleucid rulers had made similar claims for themselves in the past. To the pious Jew such a claim was altogether blasphemous.

But tyranny was not confined to the actions of foreign rulers. Their own Jewish rulers, successors to the Maccabees, come in for severe strictures. Alexander Jannaeus is a case in point. Not only did he assume the title of 'king' (unlike those who had gone before him), he desecrated his office of high priest and acted ruthlessly in his dealings with his family and the people. The result was civil war in which, with the help of foreign mercenaries, he slew no fewer than fifty thousand of his fellow Jews.

The apocalyptists believed deeply that there was a moral factor at work in history and that, accordingly, there is a judg-

ment upon history and the world's rulers which is inevitable
and decisive. That judgment falls on individuals and institutions, on nation and state, on people and kings. They would
have agreed that it falls most heavily on those, societies and
rulers alike, who imagine themselves to be gods, 'who fly in the
face of Providence and history, who put their trust in man-
made systems and worship the work of their own hands'.[8]

To the apocalyptists, their rulers' misuse of power revealed
itself, from the point of view of religion, in pride and arrogance
which were an offence against the majesty of God; and, from
the point of view of society, in cruelty and injustice which were
an offence against the moral holiness of God. They proved the
truth of the adage that 'power corrupts; and absolute power
corrupts absolutely'. The judgment of God on such rulers
and on the institutions they represented must follow as
inevitably as night follows day. Their portrayal of that judgment may be grotesque and bizarre, but the truth they em-
phasize remains, that there is a moral factor in history and
(they would say) beyond history which brings its own judgment which is both sure and terrible.

In our own generation the testimony of the Confessional
Church in Germany together with the writings and life-story
of Dietrich Bonhoeffer are a clear reminder of the tyranny of
the state in interfering with the life and witness of the church
and in establishing loyalties and moral standards which again
and again denied the tenets of the Christian gospel. Equally
eloquent are the writings of Alexander Solzhenitsyn, André
Sakharov and many other dissidents who, by reason of their
religious or political dissent, have brought down upon their
heads the condemnation of the state.

The modern church, in such circumstances as these, has
much in common with the early church which in turn had
much in common with the Jewish community from which it
sprang. But no longer was their problem simply that of the
people of God in Old Testament times – a righteous remnant
living within the community of the covenant; rather it was that

13

of a small community professing what they believed to be the true religion within a much larger community professing a false religion. The conclusion to which the early church came was that the state is a divine creation and as such has divine sanction. It is an instrument whereby justice and righteousness may be established and disaster averted. In so far as it neglects to carry out these duties, it betrays its true function. But in so far as it fulfils them, the church has an obligation to support the state as it seeks to preserve that condition of law and order which makes it possible for society to function properly and for the church adequately to do its God-given work.

But no act of injustice, however patriotic, can pass the judgment seat of God. To pervert justice or to encourage injustice is to flout the moral authority of God and to deny his right to reign. And the supreme act of sacrilege is committed, as Karl Barth reminds us, when the state demands from its subjects not simply obedience but love.[9] By abusing its divine sanction, the state becomes demonic and sets itself up in opposition to God. As Reinhold Niebuhr puts it, 'It belongs to the devil precisely because it claims to be God'.[10] This is true whether it expresses itself in the form of a deified ruler or a deified institution, in the form of a *Divus Caesar* or a *Dea Roma*. 'The worship of a Roman Empire as Divus Caesar', writes Arnold Toynbee, 'does not suffer from the remoteness, impersonalness and aloofness that are the weaknesses of its worship as Dea Roma.'[11] But each comes equally under the judgment of God.

The apostle Paul, among others, recognized the legitimate function of the state and taught submission to the lawful authorities (cf. Rom. 13.1f., 5f.). But when the era of persecution began and Christians were forced by the state to accept laws which were contrary to their convictions, it was an apocalyptic writer among them who saw in the state an expresssion of Antichrist (cf. Rev. 13) and indicated that 'the beast' whose number is 666 was none other than Nero himself. There were no doubt many at that time – as there still are in our time – who would have subscribed to the words of Peter Crassus of a later era: 'Render unto Caesar the things that are Caesar's, but not unto Tiberius the things that are Tiberius's; for Caesar is good, but Tiberius is bad.' Now as then the church has to balance Paul's words, 'Every subject must obey the government authority', over against those of Peter before the Jewish Sanhedrin, 'We ought to obey God rather than men.'

6 *Human rights*

The expression 'human rights' is a relatively modern term, but the human situation which it highlights is common to almost every generation and had a particular significance during the period when Jewish apocalyptic began to make its influence felt. The mass deportation of conquered peoples, for example, is alluded to on many occasions during the Old Testament period and this policy continued under the successors to Alexander the Great. But it was in the time of Antiochus Epiphanes that there appeared the greatest challenge to the human rights of the Jewish people and to the practice of their religion and which coloured and determined the character of much apocalyptic writing from that time forward.

It is of significance that what began as political action soon began to express itself in terms of religious persecution. In the eyes of the governing powers these two could hardly be distinguished from each other. To Antiochus, the trouble was insurrection and this he refused to tolerate. The Jewish people refused to accept his nominee Menelaus. This was an act of open rebellion which had to be quashed. Accordingly Antiochus attacked Jerusalem, reinstated Menelaus and let his soldiers loose among the people. Still as a political reprisal, he desecrated the temple and plundered its treasures. The following year (168 BC) he returned to Jerusalem determined not to allow another outbreak of insurrection. Many more were slain or carried off as slaves. The city walls were razed to the ground; the western citadel opposite the temple was strengthened and fortified and occupied by foreign troops. Irresponsible elements in the citadel shed much innocent blood and in this were aided and abetted by Jewish Hellenizers who now, by reason of advantageous taxation laws, found themselves in a highly favoured position. Many pious orthodox Jews found things too much for them and felt compelled to flee from the city of their fathers.

At this point state politics and religion began to mix inextricably. The Syrian soldiers in the citadel who worshipped *Baal Shamen* ('Lord of heaven'), already popular in the syncretistic faith of the time, took over the temple precincts for their own purposes. Soon the God of Israel was being worshipped together with and as an expression of heathen deities. Menelaus and his fellow-Hellenizers were apparently content that this should be so and gave their support to these trends.

Antiochus realized that his political programme, expressed in terms of Hellenization, was quite incompatible with the religion of Israel and the traditional worship of the temple, and so he sought to achieve his political ends by means of religious subversion. In 167 BC he issued a decree forbidding the Jewish people any more to live according to their ancestral laws (cf. I Macc. 1.41ff.; II Macc. 6.1ff.). His objective was the complete destruction and abolition of the Jewish religion. Traditional sacrifices were prohibited and sabbath observance forbidden. Children must no longer be circumcised; the scriptures in the form of scrolls of the law must be destroyed. Anyone found acting in breach of the new law would be sentenced to death. Altars to foreign gods were set up throughout the land (cf. I Macc. 1.47); Jews were forced on pain of death to offer unclean sacrifices and to eat swine's flesh (cf. II Macc. 6.18). To crown everything, in December 167 BC Antiochus introduced into the Jerusalem temple the worship of the Olympian Zeus, erecting on the altar of burnt offerings another altar bearing the image of Zeus and having, apparently, the features of Antiochus himself. It is this altar, on which swine's flesh was ordered to be offered (cf. II Macc. 6.2), which the apocalyptist Daniel calls 'the abomination that makes desolate' (11.31, 12.11).

The 'mob' then ran riot, as so often before and since,

backed up by the rough Syrian soldiers. Acts of sensuality and drunken orgies took place within the sacred precincts. Faithful Jews were forced to offer sacrifices in honour of the king's birthday and to join in the drunken procession in honour of the god Bacchus (cf. II Macc. 6.3–7). Some acquiesced; others submitted only after great heart-searching; others again chose to die rather than profane the holy covenant (cf. I Macc.1.63). Syrian agents pursued those who fled the city, molesting and threatening them in a determined attempt to stamp out the Jewish faith once and for all.

Such an account has surely a modern ring about it and tells graphically the story of molestation and persecution under the rule of fascism or communism or neo-colonialism. The account is an accurate one, in present-day terms, even down to details – desecration of synagogues or church buildings, abolition of sacred festivals, forced acceptance of foreign creeds, prohibition against teaching children the faith, confiscation of the scriptures, molestation of the faithful by state agents, long terms of imprisonment for breach of 'the civil law', and the replacement of God by 'gods' who are symbols of the state and who, at times, have appeared to wear a human face.

Racial discrimination is one devilish manifestation of all this, not least in the shape of the doctrine of *apartheid*. So also is the prevalence of torture as a normal means of government and of maintaining law and order. Penalties meted out to political and religious dissenters have already been alluded to and are a marked feature of our generation. Many hope that the so-called Helsinki Agreement will pave the way for better relations and a more secure future for the rights of ordinary citizens in many lands.

Christians and Jews have had their fair share – some would say more than their fair share – of suffering and persecution and have for a long time been in the forefront of those who have striven for human rights – not for themselves only but for all men, whatever their religion or creed, whether they be Christian, Jewish, agnostic or atheist. Wherever any individual or group of human beings is deprived of human dignity (in the form, say, of racial discrimination) or of human freedom (by charges of literary, scientific or religious 'deviation') it is the bounden duty of the Christian church to oppose such oppression even at considerable risk to itself. Bonhoeffer's words are relevant at this point: 'I cannot sing psalms in the Gregorian mode with those who do not also cry out for the Jews.' To make the excuse that 'politics and Christianity don't mix' is to be blind to the fact that in respect of human rights they cannot be separated and that in respect of human suffering all men are brothers.

In modern times societies have arisen which are altogether unlike the Jewish–Christian tradition which, for so many centuries, has characterized Western civilization. Traditional rights and age-long assumptions cannot any longer be taken for granted – such as those adumbrated in Thomas Jefferson's famous words: 'We hold these truths to be self-evident that all men are created equal; that they are endowed by their Creator with inalienable Rights.' In the light of modern society and the claims of the modern state these rights are perhaps not as self-evident or as inalienable as the fathers of the American Revolution imagined them to be. It remains as true today as ever that 'the price of liberty is eternal vigilance'.

7 Violence and the pursuit of justice

The struggle for freedom and human rights raises the further question of the use of violence in opposing oppression and establishing justice. Two kinds of violence are sometimes indicated and distinguished from each other – the violence that enslaves and the violence that liberates. The Jewish people were faced squarely with the first of these, not only in the time of Antiochus, but also during the reigns of their own Hasmonean rulers and subsequently under the Romans.

In 168 BC Antiochus sent his general Apollonius, leader of his Mysian mercenaries, to attack Jerusalem. This he did on the sabbath day when he knew that the orthodox Jews would refuse to fight (cf. I Macc. 1.29–35; II Macc. 5.23–26). The same tactic was adopted on at least one other occasion (cf. I Macc. 2.36). The action, or inaction, of the Jews was not due to any belief in 'pacifism', but to their deeply felt religious scruples about sabbath observance.

There was certainly no doubt in the minds of the Maccabees and their followers on this score. They had been subjected to a tyranny and oppression of such dimensions that it cried out for opposition by a call to arms. The Maccabean War indeed has about it the feel of a holy war. At an early stage Mattathias and his sons of the Maccabean family were joined by the Hasidim (Hasideans) whose attachment to the cause brought to it no small encouragement (cf. I Macc. 2.42). These Hasidim were among those who refused to fight on the sabbath, and for this reason it has generally been assumed that they were quietists intent only on religious, as distinct from political and national, reforms. This is now seen to be wrong. In II Maccabees, for example, they are described as 'mighty warriors of Israel' (cf. I Macc. 2.42) who 'keep up war and stir up sedition' among the Syrians (cf. II Macc. 14.6). It was they who formed the backbone of the guerrilla movement which marked the early stages of the revolt (cf. I Macc. 2.44–48). 'They rescued the law out of the hands of the Gentiles and kings, and they never let the sinner gain the upper hand' (I Macc. 2.48).

As we have seen, the author of the book of Daniel was in all probability a member of the Hasidim. Be that as it may, the book itself reflects the feelings of the Hasidic party of that time. Force was necessary to resist evil. But it had to be acknowledged that the resistance movement to which they had given their support was only 'a little help' (11.34). Salvation would come from God alone.

This reflects the convictions of the Qumran Covenanters as expressed in the so-called Dead Sea Scrolls in whom many scholars see the spiritual successors of the Hasidim. There,

VIOLENCE & APOCALYPSE

particularly in the War Scroll, we see depicted a fight to the end between 'the children of light' and 'the children of darkness' with whom are associated a righteous Israel and the evil forces of the Gentiles. In the book of Revelation we read of the pitched battle of Armageddon (cf. 16.16) and of the great city Babylon being thrown down to rise no more (cf. 18.21). Violence, human and divine, is written into almost every apocalyptic writing and is antecedent to the establishment of the kingdom of God.

It is with reference to violence and the use of violence that the word 'apocalyptic' is perhaps most widely (and most loosely) used at this present time. Ours is an era in which violence has erupted, not just in the form of wars and civil wars, but also in the form of civil strife of many and diverse kinds. On the one hand, civil rights movements have sought to follow the line of non-violence; on the other hand, revolutionary movements have resorted to the persuasion of the gun. 'Freedom marchers' and 'freedom fighters' have, in more than one country, highlighted the problem with which democracy generally and Christians in particular find themselves faced.

It was in such circumstances as these that Jewish apocalyptic sprang to birth and Christian apocalyptic first became evident. The same spirit of despair and hope prevails today and provides conditions in which the same aspirations are expressed by religious and secular writers alike.

II

From Creation to Consummation

1 *The interpretation of apocalyptic*

The purpose of this chapter is to examine, within restricted limits, the message of the ancient Jewish apocalyptists, particularly as that message throws light on their understanding of history and the end of history and our own understanding of it today.

One obvious difficulty in a study of this kind is the use of the word 'apocalyptic' itself, which is notoriously difficult to define, and which is used in modern literature, secular and religious alike, with a whole variety of meaning and frequently simply as a synonym for the word 'cataclysmic'. This ambiguity will be recognized in this chapter and the context of the word allowed to provide its own guidelines as to its particular meaning.

Thus Eduard Stauffer defines apocalyptic in terms of a pre-Christian theology of history characterized by four things: primordiality, conflict, eschatology and universalism. Human history and cosmic history belong together in the unfolding of the great dramatic conflict between the kingdom of God and the kingdom of Satan. The era of conflict will be hard and bitter but will soon be over. God's triumph is assured, and with it the triumph of God's people. It will come not by evolution but by revolution – or rather by a supernatural and catastrophic intervention. God himself will break in upon history in a mighty act of judgment and establish his kingdom. This notion of 'the end' is a constantly recurring theme in this literature. It is the end that gives meaning to the present and the past and in which all things, on earth and in heaven, will receive their deserved reward.

Klaus Koch agrees with Ringgren in defining apocalyptic as 'speculation which – often in allegorical form . . . aims to interpret the course of history and to reveal the end of the world',[12] and identifies the themes of apocalyptic in eight groups of *motifs* as follows: an urgent expectation of the impending overthrow of all earthly conditions in the immediate future; the end as a vast cosmic catastrophe; the relation of the end-time to the previous history of mankind and of the cosmos; angels and demons; catastrophe followed by salvation; the enthronement of God and the coming of his kingdom; the appearance of a mediator/redeemer with royal functions; and the glory of the age to come.[13]

Harvey Cox, commenting on its modern secularized expression, says:

> Apocalypse creates a mood of world negation, fatalism, retreat from earthly chores, and sometimes even a virulent otherwordliness . . . No earthly goals are worth holding since they are equally corrupt or illusory . . . Rational action is useless because powers outside history and beyond human control will quickly bring the whole thing to a blazing end.[14]

This judgment, I believe, however apposite it may be for some, would be less than fair if applied to the ancient apocalyptists who, as we shall see, were not as negative or as fatalistic as Harvey Cox's words imply.

The extravagances of interpretation often indulged in and the excesses to which these ancient apocalyptic books have led have caused many to look askance at them and to downgrade them as unworthy and degenerate survivals of ancient prophecy of Old Testament times. Thus, R. T. Herford[15] describes apocalyptic as a dangerous influence, the product of weak minds and unbalanced judgments, while G. F. Moore[16] warns against contaminating the religion of Judaism with such writings. This is, I believe, to do a grave injustice to writers who were counted among 'the wise' and 'the righteous' and to their teachings which, despite their extravagant and esoteric language, deeply influenced the early church and have brought such assurance to Christians in many generations.

In times of stress and persecution, such as our own, the books of Daniel and Revelation, for example, have taken on a new importance and have provided a quarry from which the faithful have often hewn new hopes and fresh assurance for the days in which they are living, identifying the Antichrist with their oppressors and persecutors and pointing forward to the imminent return of Christ and the establishment of his kingdom of righteousness and peace. In this way Christians have identified a long line of tyrants from Nero to Hitler; some indeed have sold their all and have waited with bated breath for the consummation of all things, the *eschaton* when God's rule will begin, the wicked will be judged and the righteous enter into their God-given heritage. Writing as a pastor and preacher in Germany during the traumatic years of Hitler's regime, Walter Lüthi makes this pertinent comment:

> Daniel contains a particular message for our time, often in a very startling way ... We are not dealing here with a burnt-out crater. Daniel is an active volcano. Therefore if anyone thinks that it is a matter of playing with cold lava, for edification or otherwise, he should realize he is playing with fire.[17]

In theological circles, as distinct from popular expectation, there has also been a revival of interest in apocalyptic in recent years not least, as we have seen, in the writings of Käsemann and Pannenberg and, we may add, of Moltmann. Ernst Käsemann, indeed, goes so far as to say that 'apocalyptic was the mother of all Christian theology'.[18] Wolfhart Pannenberg sees its value in the light it casts on the nature of history which is to be understood only in the light of its consummation.

Jürgen Moltmann, in his *Theology of Hope* (see page 31 below), interprets its significance in terms of the world's final destiny.

Among writers on the secular scene the recurring themes of violence, violation of human rights, pressure to conform etc. are often expressed in apocalyptic terms, the chief difference being that the mundane takes the place of the supra-mundane and revelation is sometimes seen to express itself in revolution. More will be said of this later. Here we simply note, in modern theological and secular literature alike, the occurrence and reinterpretation of the apocalyptic theme.

2 *History and contemporaneity*

It is often alleged that the apocalyptists have no ultimate concern for history as such, but are interested in it only in so far as it leads up to and is a preparation for the end when God will set all wrongs right and vindicate his people in the eyes of the world. Such a statement, however, requires qualification and clearer definition. George Caird in this connection makes a helpful distinction between *das Ende* and *die Endzeit*: 'To expect the End is not the same as to expect an End time. The one is an event beyond which nothing can conceivably happen. The other is a period of indefinite duration in which much is expected to happen.'[19] He concludes that what the Jewish people expected was not *das Ende* but *die Endzeit*. Such a distinction is valid, but I myself would prefer to define *das Ende* in terms of the transcendental and the end of history, and *die Endzeit* in terms of the temporal and the continuation of history and to say that in apocalyptic thought there is a fluctuation between the one and the other and, at times, a mingling and merging of these two concepts.

It is true that for some at least of the apocalyptists, the breaking in of the end means the close of history as we know it, and the 'stuff' from which history is made is not truly characteristic of the kingdom that is yet to be. The dualistic view of the world, for example, set out in some at least of these books, finds expression in a doctrine of two ages in which 'this age' is set over against 'the age to come' and in which 'eternity' is divorced from history. History ceases to be the substance of the kingdom. The kingdom, on which the future hope is focused, takes on a transcendental character and points beyond earth to heaven. 'Talk about history,' writes Hendrikus Berkhof, 'is talk about consummation' and 'to talk about consummation is to talk about a break'.[20] It is that transcendent and other-worldly kingdom that really matters, and it is to that kingdom that the whole of history moves and in which it finds its fulfilment.

It would be wrong, however, to conclude that to the apocalyptists as a whole history is unimportant and the events of history have no eternal significance. It is true that allusions to history and contemporary event are often obscure. As in photography, so also in the apocalyptic vision, when the focus is on eternity the immediate foreground lacks clarity and definition. Apocalyptic encompasses everything from creation to consummation, but because its focus is fixed on that consummation contemporary event lacks precision. It is concealed behind obscure imagery and is made difficult to recognize by reason, for example, of the phenomenon of pseudonymity which casts the present into the future, giving it at times an air of unreality. Allusions to people and places are often cryptic and tantalizingly obscure. Nevertheless continuity remains, and history as well as eternity has a firm place within the revelation of God's purpose made known to them. The contemporary scene is the stage on which the divine purpose is even now being worked out and it is in contemporary terms that the kingdom is to be understood.

This is hardly surprising for, as we have already observed, much of this literature was born out of the religious persecution and political intrigue of Palestine and the Dispersion during the greatly troubled inter-testamental period. Indeed, there is good reason to believe that the revolutionary Zealots may well have found in its teaching ready fuel for their fire, and that this was one of the factors which explain its esoteric character and its careful handling over the years by the synagogue, the church and the state.

This continuity between the 'here' and the 'hereafter' is to be seen also in the way in which some apocalyptic writers at any rate interpreted the nature of the coming kingdom. In certain earlier books such as Daniel, I Enoch 83–90 and the Psalms of Solomon the writers equate the coming kingdom with the golden age and envisage it as being established here on earth as the final phase of history. It will be heralded by the judgment in which evil-doers will be destroyed and the enemies of God's people will be punished. Even the dead will be raised in their bodies to share in this earthly, albeit eternal, kingdom. The blessing of the kingdom will be both material and spiritual; it will register both the religious and the political fulfilment of their nation's dreams. There are, it is true, idealistic elements in the descriptions of this coming kingdom; but it is essentially an earthly kingdom ruled over by God or his Messiah under whom the Gentiles will be made to serve. It is the stuff from which history is made and by which the kingdom is built.

In several of the later books the messianic kingdom is distinguished from the age to come and takes the form of a temporary kingdom on earth to be followed by a timeless eternity in heaven. The kingdom still belongs to this present age and marks the *climax* of history. At its end the dead are raised for judgment; then is inaugurated the final age beyond history in which all earthly wrongs are set right by the retributive justice of God.

These illustrations show that, whereas often in apocalyptic thought the break between history and eternity is decisive, the kingdom continued to be regarded by many as belonging to the contemporary world and not to be separated from the common stuff of history. In the light of this I would wish to qualify as a general statement the words of Harvey Cox when he writes: 'Apocalypticism and politics are inherently incompatible . . . Apocalypticism is at work wherever people simply decide to opt out of the political process and seek personal salvation or wait for the deluge.'[21] It is true, as we shall see, that in the apocalyptic literature prominence is given to the destiny of the individual and to 'personal salvation' in the age to come; but the overall perspective is still that of the community − be it the righteous remnant or the nation or the righteous gathered out of all mankind − and the objective of salvation is the creation of a new society in which righteousness and peace and, indeed, all the marks of good government and right rule are supreme. The promised kingdom is one of *shalom* and as such is not altogether divorced from earth or history or from the kingdoms of men. Its sign is that of justice and peace − not just in some far-off time or place, but in the struggles of contemporary life.

It is of interest in this connection to observe the fairly frequent use of the word 'apocalyptic' in the writings of present-day 'liberation theologians' and the relation they see to exist between the coming kingdom and contemporary historical and political event. More often than not the word is used very loosely to refer to the political struggle for liberation or else is confused with the word 'eschatology' and relates simply to the nature of the coming 'new society'. Nevertheless, it is not altogether without significance that the term is in fact used in such a context, for its use here reflects, in part at least, the mood and aspirations of the apocalyptic 'liberation' writers of the time of Antiochus or during the reigns of the Hasmoneans, of Herod and of Nero.

Thus, Gustavo Gutierrez speaks about the importance of eschatology 'as the driving force of a future-oriented history' which is 'inseparably joined with its historical contemporaneity and urgency'. And again, 'One must be extremely careful not to replace a Christianity of the Beyond with a Christianity of the Future; if the former tended to forget the world, the latter runs the risk of neglecting a miserable and unjust present and the struggle for liberation.' What he has in mind is an eschatology in which 'the future promises conflicts and confrontations, a struggle to become free from the forces which enslave men and exploit social classes'. This is altogether different, he adds, from that eschatology which 'expressed the wish for a disengagement of the Christian faith from the forces of this world; the basis for this was a lack of interest in terrestrial realities and a historical pessimism which discouraged any attempts at great tasks'.[22] The apocalyptists, in their interpretation of eschatology, would have understood the references to 'conflicts and confrontations' and to the 'struggle to become free' from powers which enslave and exploit and some at least would have recognized the terrestrial limits placed on the future hope. Not all of them, however, would have been happy with the stress sometimes laid on the importance of political revolution to achieve their end. The real power, they would say, lies in the hands of God who is the Lord of history and ruler of the nations of the earth, who will destroy tyrants and break their kingdoms in pieces. In his own time and in his own way he will establish his kingdom and, on earth or in heaven, cause the wrath of man to praise him.

3 History and the divine purpose

For the apocalyptists history and event had meaning, however, not simply in terms of rulers, armies and empires, but preeminently in terms of the eternal purpose of God and his control over all the affairs of men. It is sometimes alleged that they were pessimists who wrote off the happenings of this life as having no worth and no meaning except in so far as they prepared the faithful for the life beyond; that they despaired of their lot and lived for the time when God would blot out the universe and usher in a new heaven and a new earth.

It is true that they believed things were going from bad to worse, that the present world order was corrupt and ripe for destruction and that the time was near at hand when evil would be destroyed and evil men punished for their sin. It is true too that they despaired of men ever being able to effect their own salvation or bring about their own deliverance. But such despair is only one side of the coin, the other side of which is hope. By their writings they added their weight to the cause of liberation, but they never doubted – even in the darkest days of persecution – that God himself was in control of their affairs and indeed of the whole panorama of human history. Tyrants might rule, but it was only by the permissive will of God. The rise and fall of empires were in the control of one in whose hands lay the final victory and in whose triumph and kingdom they would have a glorious part. That kingdom, as we have seen, is sometimes conceived of as being 'in heaven'; at other times it is well and truly on this earth. Whatever be its shape, its coming is in the hands of God and that is what matters supremely. They were men of vision and of faith who were pleased to see the happenings of history in the light of eternity, to interpret the affairs of men in terms of the divine purpose and who saw meaning in history because at the end of the process lay the goal, foreordained and predetermined by God, in the light of which the whole of history would at last make sense. They were interested and involved in the process of history, both past and present; but its real significance for them lay in the fact of its completion and fulfilment in the kingdom. The great Seleucid and Ptolemaic dynasties, for example, whose power seemed invincible, are shown, says Edwin Bevan, as 'phases in a world-process whose end is the kingdom of God'.[23] They based this conviction on their faith in God who 'rules the kingdom of men and gives it to whom he will' (Dan. 4.17).

They might understand the coming of the kingdom in terms of the end-time when God's powerful and just reign would be recognized within history by men and nations or in terms of the end, when the earth and the heavens would fold up and an eternal, transcendent order would be brought into being. In either case its coming and the whole course of history is under the control of the eternal, prevailing purpose of Almighty God. For this reason they were essentially men of hope, whose confidence was set in God who, as in the case of Daniel, was able to deliver them out of the burning fiery furnace (cf. Dan. 3.17) and to deliver the kingdom to the saints of the Most High (cf. Dan. 7.18).

This endeavour to understand and evaluate historical event in the light of the consummation has found expression, as already noted, in the writings of Wolfhart Pannenberg, who has done much to reinstate apocalyptic as a class of literature worthy of careful study by Christian theologians. History in process is not self-explanatory but becomes comprehensible only in the light of the finalization of that process. 'Revelation is not comprehended completely in the beginning, but at the end of the revealing history.'[24] Within and beyond history stands one who gives meaning and purpose to the whole. From the vantage point of the consummation men will see the working out of the divine purpose and recognize his handiwork in history and in all creation.

The apocalyptists would have agreed – and also disagreed – with Gutierrez when he writes,

It has often been noted that a characteristic of contemporary man is that he lives in terms of tomorrow, oriented towards the future, fascinated by what does not yet exist. The spiritual condition of today's man is more and more determined by the model of the man of tomorrow ... He is outgrowing his present condition and entering a new era, a world ... fashioned by his own hands ... History is no longer as it was for the Greeks, an *anamnesis*, a remembrance. It is rather a thrust into the future. The contemporary world is full of latent possibilities and expectations.[25]

They would have agreed with him that the key to the present lies in the future and that the expectations of the new era are both exciting and pressing. But they would not have understood his vagueness concerning the nature of the coming kingdom or his reference to its erection by men's hands or his emphasis that the contemporary world is necessarily the primary focus of reference. To them the architect of all things is God who, in the beginning, created the universe and who, at last, will bring it to completion. He is involved in the historical process, but he is not so historicized as to lose his otherness. So it is also with his kingdom. He is the transcendent God whose kingdom breaks in from beyond and gives meaning to history which can truly be understood only in the light of eternity.

Jürgen Moltmann, in his exposition of the theology of hope, finds in this very fact of discontinuity between historical reality and future promise a significant contribution on the part of the apocalyptic writers. 'Without apocalyptic,' he writes, 'a theological eschatology remains bogged down in the ethnic history of men or the existential history of the individual.'[26] The thing that denies the present and its tale of tragedy and woe is the promise of what is to be. Or, to put it another way, the transcendent hope makes man aware of the pain of the present and gives content and meaning to everything that is.

The theology of the apocalyptists, to use our modern jargon, is in this sense a 'theology of hope' as well as a 'theology of liberation'. 'In the theology of hope,' writes Orlando E. Costas, 'hope is basically apocalyptic. It irrupts into the present from a God who is always ahead.'[27] The future holds the key to the present; history finds meaning in eternity; the purpose of God gives continuity to both and the assurance of the establishment of his kingdom of righteousness and peace.

This teaching of the apocalyptists concerning the understanding of history in terms of the consummation and of all things in terms of the divine purpose can bear confident comparison with other ideologies familiar to present-day society – the revolutionary hope of Marxism, the liberating hope of existentialism or the pragmatic hope of the social sciences. These men of faith assert with conviction that God himself is

the ground of hope, that his purpose for mankind will reach its
fulfilment and that the certainty of that fulfilment gives meaning to life both here and hereafter.

4 *The unity of history*

The apocalyptist, then, saw the working out of the divine
purpose within and beyond history. But more than that, they
saw it in the whole of history and indeed in the whole of the
cosmos. Believing that they stood very near to the consummation, they were able to take in the whole of history at a glance
and see it in its entirety *sub specie aeternitatis*. Past, present and
future formed a continuous perspective. Their concept of time
and of the passing of time was sometimes confused, as
Edmond Jacob observes concerning the vision in Daniel 2:
'The unfolding of history is of little importance . . . the four
empires which come one after another are all present at the
end of the last empire.'[28] But more important than the continuity of history was its wholeness, a wholeness which is seen in
perspective only from the point of view of the consummation.
Such perspective shows God's purpose for individuals and for
nations alike. But it goes beyond even these, for the whole
universe is his concern. The history of the cosmos as well as
the history of mankind is involved in his eternal purpose. All
events and all created things will find their fulfilment and
meaning in terms of the single goal towards which everything
is moving – the coming of God's kingdom in which his eternal
purpose will find its vindication.

It is easily imagined that this idea of the unity of history is a
modern notion in keeping with the shrinking of the universe
through the ease of travel and the concept of the world as 'a
global village'. It was, in fact, inherited from the early church,
which taught that all men are 'one in Christ Jesus' (Gal. 3.28)
and that the whole of history is made one through God's
purpose in him. But the idea did not originate even there. It
goes back through the Jewish apocalyptists to the Old

Testament prophets as evidenced especially in the writings of Deutero-Isaiah. The unity of history is a corollary of the unity of God. The monotheistic faith (which finds explicit reference in the prophet of the exile) finds inevitable expression in the all-embracing purpose of Almighty God. This is reflected earlier still, in the book of Amos, where the rise and fall of nations is in the control of God who unites all history in a single plan.

It was left to the apocalyptists, however, to complete the logic of the prophets' belief and to work it out in terms of their own historical situation and of their conviction concerning the fast-approaching consummation. This they did by setting out history systematically in schemes which they worked out with mathematical precision. The affairs of men and nations, from creation to consummation, are divided and sub-divided into ages or aeons, each with its own characteristics and each with its own predetermined span. As the writer's gaze sweeps over the past and (in the form of prophetic forecast) explains the present he can point with assurance to the future which is already here.

This, indeed, is the abiding message of apocalyptic – not its schematizations of history and not its prognostications, but rather its assurances that the long course of history, in which God has been at work, will reach its glorious climax when the eternal purposes of God will find their fulfilment and he will reign in his kingdom as Lord over all. The end is at hand; the consummation of all history is within the sight of faith: 'For the youth of the world is past, and the strength of the creation is already exhausted, and the advent of the times is very short, yea, they have passed by; and the pitcher is near to the cistern, and the ship to the port, and the course of the journey to the city, and life to consummation' (II Bar. 85.10).

5 Re-creation and redemption

The popular Old Testament view of the future hope with its military leader and its earthly kingdom continued to hold a secure place in the popular imagination. But from the time of Daniel onwards there is, in Jewish apocalyptic writings, an obvious tension between this outlook and a new kind of eschatology which corresponds in some ways at least to the tension between the Messiah and the Son of man. It is an eschatology which, in the words of Mowinckel, is at once 'dualistic, cosmic, universalistic, transcendental and individualistic'.[29] No longer are God's enemies confined to men of flesh and blood; they are the demonic powers of darkness entrenched in God's vast universe and in men's hearts. No longer are God's battles to be fought with sword and spear; they now assume cosmic proportions and involve all created things. Thus apocalyptic eschatology becomes more and more transcendent, with stress from first to last on the supernatural and the supramundane. Deliverance will come, not through men, but from God himself, who will bring in his kingdom and usher in the age to come, which will mark the triumph of his eternal purpose.

What is more, in this promised hope and in this coming kingdom the creation itself will share. The usurped creation (taken over by evil forces) will be restored; the corrupted universe will be cleansed; the created world will be re-created. Two 're-creation motifs' run through much apocalyptic thinking. One is that the end will in some way correspond to the beginning. What the Creator willed and planned at the time of creation he will redeem, rectify and restore, bringing to perfection what he has already made. The other is that of paradise or the heavenly Jerusalem which, like paradise itself, has been prepared beforehand by God at the beginning of his creation. Sometimes, as we have seen, it is portrayed as earthly in character and at other times it is 'heavenly' and transcendental. The God who acts and saves in history is the same God who acts and saves in creation. God the Creator and God the Redeemer are one. The kingdom is the completion of all his works.

The redemption of the cosmos and the redemption of

human history belong together in the one saving purpose of God. A hint of this connection is given in the common notion in these writings that the six days of creation followed by the seventh day of rest correspond to the long course of world history to be followed by the promised kingdom. The beginning of creation, moreover, marks the beginning of the historical process and together they will share in the final redemption. Jürgen Moltmann writes:

> Historic eschatology is here struggling with cosmology and ... makes the cosmos understandable ... The 'universe' is no longer, as in pagan cosmology, a thing to be interpreted in astromythical or pantheistic or mechanistic terms as the sum total of the world and of our satisfaction with it. Instead, it splits into aeons in the apocalyptic process – into a world that is coming and one that is passing away ... The whole world is now involved in God's eschatological process of history, not only the world of men and nations.[30]

Here again it is 'the world that is coming' that holds the key to creation and cosmos as it does to human history. What André Dumas says of biblical time in this connection is equally true of apocalyptic thought: 'Biblical time', he says, 'is the advance of creation towards an eschatology, of a seed towards its blossoming, of a promise towards its accomplishment. Biblical time is neither cyclical, nor regressive, but messianic.'[31] The messianic kingdom, with or without an actual Messiah, is the goal of all history and all creation.

6 *The powers of evil*

It becomes clear from a study of this literature that one of the most pressing problems facing the apocalyptic writers is the existence in the world of moral evil. The several theories that are propounded in these books concerning the origin of evil need not concern us here except to remark that, in the popular imagination, it was bound up with possession by demons who were the evil progeny of the unlawful union between the fallen angels called 'Watchers' and the 'daughters of men'. The account is based on the story in Gen. 6.1–4 and is developed in I Enoch, the book of Jubilees and elsewhere. It is these evil spirits who encourage men to wage war against one another and to enslave their brothers, leading them on 'to do all manner of wrong and sin, and all manner of transgressions, to corrupt and destroy, and to shed blood on the earth' (Jub. 11.5). Even inanimate nature is not immune. To their solicitations is due the corruption of mankind and indeed of the whole world. This evil in these writings affects not only the souls of men, but the entire created universe. It assumes cosmic dimensions and awaits a redemption in which not only men and society but the whole animate and inanimate creation as well will share.

For of this the apocalyptists were sure, that in the end evil will be utterly destroyed. The dramatic conflict between the *civitas dei* and the *civitas diaboli*, which has been going on from the very beginning of the world and which has swept up into its toils men and beasts and all created things, will reach its great climax. The powers of evil will make their last desperate attempt to overthrow the forces of good. Sin and wickedness will do their worst before God's kingdom is established and the end comes. In 'the mystery to come', writes the author of the Qumran Book of Mysteries, '. . . wickedness shall be banished by righteousness as darkness is banished by the light. As smoke clears and is no more, so shall wickedness perish for ever and righteousness be revealed like a sun . . .'[32] Both here and throughout the whole apocalyptic literature, beneath the bizarre and often crude imagery, there lies this firm conviction concerning the moral character of God whose holy and righteous purpose will at last be vindicated.

Closely associated with these 'signs of the end' is the figure of Antichrist who, it is believed, will appear in the last days to do battle with God himself. Sometimes he appears as a human being, at other times as the embodiment of the prince of wickedness, Beliar, the leader of the hosts of iniquity. In the end *all* will be routed and all creation share in the salvation of God.

Such a notion of evil, with its belief in demons and its battles between the powers of darkness and the powers of light, has little in common with the beliefs of civilized and sophisticated modern man. It is true that the practice of exorcism continues in some branches of the Christian church, but despite this most Western Christians find great difficulty in associating evil and suffering with spirit-possession. Following the example of the apostle Paul, they attempt to 'demythologize', for, though he took seriously the demonic nature of evil from which the world is to be redeemed, he no longer thought of 'principalities and powers' in terms of archons who govern the planets and the stars but rather as the sum of all those forces in the universe opposed to Christ and his church. Not all, however, are perhaps as wise in their treatment of the subject as the apostle and too readily dismiss it as mythological and mythical. It is all too easy in the process of demythologizing, however legitimate the process may be, to 'throw out the baby with the bathwater'. In discarding the form, care must be taken not to discard the content and the expression of truth it contains.

The apocalyptists would argue that it is too facile a judgment simply to say that the evil for which each man is responsible is the product of his own wilful act of sinning, for that same evil has somehow in a mysterious way became a power which affects and afflicts every member of the human race. H. H. Rowley, in a helpful passage, attempts to explain this mysterious power of evil in the world in terms of the Hebrew concept of 'corporate personality'. While recognizing that goodness and evil are personal terms and adhere only in persons, he recognizes also that we all reflect the *Zeitgeist* of our day which is not confined to living individuals or even to a large number of individuals together, but continues from generation to generation and inheres in the totality of the whole.

He goes on to use this concept to give meaning to Beliar, the prince of demons. Beliar is 'the incarnate evil of the whole in each, functioning through individuals, who are also knit together in a deep unity.' Beliar is a reminder of the sociality of evil:

If we are more than separate individuals, if we are members of a wider whole that embraces the past as well as the present, that gathers into the stream of its life each one of us and that operates through us, then a potent force of evil may be in the stream of that life, derived from individuals, but transcending individuals, though found in varying degrees in individuals. And Beliar may stand for that totality of evil beings, not alone of our day but of all days, maintaining from age to age and from generation to generation the evil which is found in the unceasing stream of evil men, the evil which is incarnated in greater or lesser measure in them all, yet which in the whole is heightened beyond any of its individual manifestations. In all our sin we are not merely ourselves sinning. We are contributing something to the vitality of Beliar.[33]

7 *Life after death*

We come finally to an area where the apocalyptists registered a considerable breakthrough in religious thought. I refer to the belief they express in the life beyond. Modern man may pretend to be blasé about death, inured as he is to war and surfeited by human holocaust. But, despite appearances, the subject still has for him a remarkable fascination, even though he himself may have no recognizable religious faith. The message of the apocalyptists, for all its crudity, has something to say in this connection that is of lasting worth, arising as it does out of a situation not altogether unlike our own. I have examined elsewhere and at some length their profound contribution at this point,[34] and need not dwell here on their developing understanding of the nature of the hereafter. I confine myself to only one or two observations.

It is true, as we have seen, that the apocalyptists still think of survival in terms of the nation and in this regard are true successors of the prophets. But their experience of suffering and persecution led them beyond this to a belief also in the survival of the individual in the life beyond. It is a strange thing that scholars speak of the development of 'individualism' in Jeremiah or in Ezekiel as a great advance in religious thought whereas in the apocalyptists it is all too often regarded as a backward step. This sense that the individual matters in the eyes of God and will share in his eternal kingdom is, I believe, a major contribution on the part of these writers. Logic and rationality are perhaps among the least of their virtues, but they took the teaching of the Old Testament to its logical conclusion and spelt out, albeit at times in fanciful and speculative language, their firm belief that God would not allow the good to perish, but would receive them at last into his kingdom.

It is of the greatest significance, moreover, that they saw survival beyond death in the form of resurrection. Their Hebrew psychology with its belief in the totality of human personality no doubt influenced their thinking in this connection. So too did their notion of the coming kingdom, which some at least expected to see established on earth. The ebb and flow in their thinking is clearly evident in their often fanciful and graphic pictures of the life beyond with its truncated souls awaiting the resurrection of the body, the divisions of heaven and the compartments of hell. There is no consistency either in their identification of those who survive death. Sometimes it is a religious *élite* from among the faithful Jews; at other times it is the righteous Israelites; at other times again it is the righteous as such, be they Jew or Gentile. Sometimes the wicked are obliterated; at other times, through resurrection or otherwise, they are made to suffer for their sins.

This concept of punishment finds its focus in the great day of judgment which has much in common with the Old Testament 'day of the Lord' but which now assumes a forensic character and takes the form of a great assize. Here again there is a great fluidity of belief concerning those who are to be judged. But, be it nation or individual, be it the Gentiles or simply 'the wicked', there is a strong ethical undertone. Moral values are the criterion of judgment, be it of nations or men or angels. Those who are judged will receive their just reward. Men are responsible for what they do or do not do; and they are responsible to God who is not only Redeemer but also Judge of all.

This chapter has attempted to paint a picture on a big canvas. It will be seen that the apocalyptists choose big subjects and paint with often garish colours. The result is not always attractive or even edifying. But, like John the Baptist, they too 'prepared the way of the Lord'. Despite their idiosyncrasies and flights of fancy they speak to us a word from God from which our modern world can still learn if it has an ear to hear.

III

Kingdom and *Kerygma*

1 *The influence of apocalyptic thought on the New Testament*

In the Preface to my book *The Method and Message of Jewish Apocalyptic* I expressed the judgment that, in the teaching of Jewish apocalyptic of the inter-testamental period, we find not only a continuation of the Old Testament but also an anticipation of the New. This literature helps to bridge the gap between the two and illustrates certain significant developments in religious belief, especially of an eschatological and messianic kind, which took place during the vital years between the two Testaments. One of these developments concerns the notion of the kingdom of God which features so prominently, in fact if not in name, in the Jewish apocalyptic writings of that time as well as in the New Testament itself, and which is a central factor in the teaching of Jesus. As Hendrikus Berkhof writes:

> It is not possible to accept the New Testament proclamation concerning the relationship of God and history without accepting in principle the related witness of the prophets and apocalypses. To a certain degree this observation holds also for the non-canonical apocalyptical literature of the inter-testamental period. It contributed to the atmosphere in which Jesus and his apostles lived and to their attention to the more apocalyptic parts of the Old Testament.[35]

Jesus was born into, and the early church grew up in, a religious atmosphere which was in fair measure influenced, if not created, by the beliefs and imaginings of the Jewish

41

apocalyptic writers whose ideas, there is good reason to believe, were much more widespread than their books.

Let me give just three illustrations of this from the New Testament. One is to be found, as we shall see more fully presently, in the teaching of Jesus and the New Testament generally concerning the kingdom as a new divine order arising out of God's final triumph over the demonic forces of evil entrenched in the universe. John, for example, reminds us that 'the whole world is in the power of the evil one' (5.19); in Luke's account of the temptation Satan claims that the world is his to dispose of as he wills (4.6); while Matthew declares that with the coming of the kingdom of God the kingdom of Satan will be broken (12.28). In the temptation narrative of Mark 1.12f., Satan is clearly depicted as the demonic prince of apocalyptic speculation. Jesus' acts of exorcism are presented as 'mopping-up operations of isolated units of Satan's hosts',[36] for the captain of the hosts of evil has already been bound hand and foot (cf. Mark 3.27). Matters reach a climax on the cross and in the resurrection when the 'principalities and powers', described as 'the rulers of this age', will be routed (cf. I Cor. 2.8).

A second illustration is to be found in the concept of the kingdom as a mystery in the synoptic gospels and in the writings of Paul. In the book of Daniel and in the extra-canonical apocalyptic books the word *mysterion* (or its Hebrew or Aramaic equivalents *sodh* or *raz*) is used to signify a divine mystery whose interpretation has been given to a select few. In the main such mysteries concern creation and re-creation and express themselves in terms of cosmology and eschatology.

These same notions prevail in the New Testament writings also, where the word *mysterion* appears with several shades of meaning, but refers particularly to an 'open secret', i.e. a divine plan concealed by God from the general run of men, but now revealed to those chosen to receive it. In Mark 4.11, for example, Jesus chooses to make known the secrets of the kingdom to the inner circle of his disciples in typically apocalyptic style: 'To you has been given the secret of the kingdom of God, but for those outside everything is in parables.' He himself is the interpreter of the mystery and not least of the scriptures which contain and conceal the hidden mysteries of God. This mystery which, according to Paul, 'was kept secret for long ages but is now disclosed' (Rom. 16.25f.) has been made known by revelation 'that through the church the manifold wisdom of God might now be made known' (Eph. 3.3, 9f.). It is the function of preaching, he implies, to make known this mystery (cf. Rom. 16.25; Eph. 3.8) which is 'Christ in you, the hope of glory' (Col. 1.26f.).

Here too the mystery is concerned with the notions of creation and re-creation. The redemption wrought by God in the coming kingdom will involve the whole created universe which will be cleansed, restored and re-created, 'for the creation waits with eager longing for the revealing of the sons of God' (Rom. 8.19).

The kingdom, like the one in whom it is embodied, will remain hidden and a mystery until its secret is revealed (cf. Mark 4.11), and is part of the 'messianic secret' of Jesus as the Son of man.

This suggests a third illustration of the influence of apocalyptic thought on the New Testament. I refer to the use by Jesus, and by others concerning him, of the title 'Son of man' and its association with the consummation and his *parousia* in glory. The occurrence and use of this expression in Daniel 7 was, I believe, a considerable factor in the thinking of Jesus and in the development of his religious consciousness. To him it meant more than simply the assumption of an Old Testament title; it meant the acceptance of the truth behind it that, as with Daniel's Son of man, so with himself there would be given to him 'dominion and glory and a kingdom' (Dan. 7.14). The great crisis of world history, foretold in the book of Daniel, had found expression in his coming and would at last be made manifest in his 'coming with the clouds of heaven' (Mark 14.62).

It is within this atmosphere of apocalyptic hope and against this background of apocalyptic expectation that 'Jesus came into Galilee, preaching the gospel of God, and saying, "The time is fulfilled, and the kingdom of God is at hand"' (Mark 1.15; cf. Dan. 2.44). The proclamation or *kerygma* of the early church, like that of its Master, was to continue the same theme and to interpret the kingdom in terms of Jesus' coming and of Jesus' coming again.

2 *The* kerygma: *the kingdom present*

In his book, *The Apostolic Preaching and its Developments*, C. H. Dodd examines the content of this primitive *kerygma*, as evidenced by Paul, the Acts of the Apostles, the other New Testament writings and the gospels themselves. It expresses itself in a fairly common pattern throughout and incorporates, in its variable forms, an essential core. Dodd describes its 'general scheme' in these words:

> It begins by proclaiming that 'this is that which was spoken by the prophets'; the age of fulfilment has dawned, and Christ is its Lord; it then proceeds to recall the historical facts, leading up to the resurrection and exaltation of Christ and the promise of his coming in glory; and it ends with the call to repentance and the offer of forgiveness.[37]

It is this same *kerygma* which forms the theme and provides the pattern for Mark's gospel, for example, and gives significance to its opening words: 'The beginning of the gospel of Jesus Christ.' The scope of the gospel indicates the content of the *kerygma*, and is reflected throughout in Jesus' own teaching and preaching: 'Jesus came into Galilee preaching the gospel of God, and saying, "The time is fulfilled, and the kingdom of God is at hand: repent and believe in the gospel"' (Mark 1.15).

'The kingdom of God', according to the synoptic gospels at any rate, was the recurring theme of Jesus' message and was bound up with the events of his life, death and resurrection. To proclaim these events is to preach the gospel of the kingdom. In him the messianic age, to which the prophets and apocalyptists had pointed, had now arrived; the great day had at last dawned; the powers of evil entrenched in the world now knew that because of him their doom was sealed.

This is seen, for example, in his teaching and in particular in so many of his parables, the burden of whose message is that in the person and in the ministry of Jesus the kingdom has truly come among men. It is seen also in his miracles, not least his miracles of healing and (as we have seen) his exorcism of evil spirits. These were more than acts of physical healing; they were at the same time demonstrations of the power and victory of God over the powers of Satan: 'If it is by the Spirit of God that I cast out demons, then the kingdom of God has come upon you' (Matt. 12.28). Similarly the miracles performed by his disciples are evident signs of the overthrow of God's archenemy: 'The seventy returned with joy, saying, "Lord, even the demons are subject to us in your name!" And he said to them, "I saw Satan fall like lightning from heaven"' (Luke 10.17f.). Such exorcisms are clear evidence that Satan's days are numbered, that he is even now being stripped of his power and that his house is already 'plundered' (cf. Matt. 12.29). Such miracles on the part of Jesus and his disciples are portrayed as expressions of a great eschatological drama in which the final victory of God over Satan is assured and which demonstrate the breaking in of the kingdom of God.

Occupying a central place in this drama were the facts of Jesus' death and resurrection. Here again the struggle with Satan, which began in the wilderness and was continued in his exorcisms, reaches its climax in the death of Jesus. Thus the apostle Paul pictures the cross as a war-chariot in which Christ 'disarmed the principalities and powers and made a public example of them, triumphing over them in it' (Col. 2.15). It is these very principalities and powers, 'the rulers of this age', who were directly responsible for the crucifixion of the Lord of glory (cf. I Cor. 2.8).

In this same connection it is surely not accidental that in all three synoptic gospels Jesus' discourses concerning the approaching judgment, which ushers in the 'day of the Lord', are followed almost immediately by the story of Christ's passion (cf. Matt. 24; Mark 13; Luke 21). The evangelists tell us of the cooling off of human love in the last days and of great oppression which will befall mankind. They foretell strange natural phenomena, such as the eclipse of the sun and an earthquake, both of which take place at the time of the crucifixion. These are the messianic woes which precede the breaking in of the great 'day of the Lord'. This Jesus, we are told, is 'a man attested to you by God with mighty works and wonders and signs' (Acts 2.22). Following the messianic woes of Gethsemane and Golgotha comes the resurrection, which for Jesus marks the beginning of the great 'day of the Lord'. The new age has dawned. The Son of man will be exalted and be seen 'coming with the clouds of heaven' (Mark 14.62). The *kerygma* declared that in him the kingdom had come, in his miracles its presence was made manifest, and in his death and resurrection it was seen to be present 'with power' (Mark 9.1; cf. Rom. 1.4). Here was the point of division between past history and the breaking in of God's rule among men. What had been prophesied in scripture had at last come true.

3 *The* kerygma: *the kingdom future*

There is ample evidence in the New Testament, however, that the coming of the kingdom is not simply a present experience bound up with the ministry, death and resurrection of Jesus; it is also a future event. Even if it be argued that there is a tendency to read back references to the *parousia*, the evidence remains unassailable that Jesus expected in the future an event, associated with his own person and triumph, by which the existing order would come to an end and that which had begun to reveal itself in his public ministry would be brought to its consummation. The language used in the gospels to describe this great event is varied – it is the consummation of all things, the coming of the kingdom 'in power', the 'day' of the Son of man and so forth. The later development of belief in the *parousia* is not to be seen as an accretion to the teaching of Jesus, but rather as something that arose directly out of it and was deeply embedded in what Jesus himself believed and taught. This is illustrated in such a passage as Mark 14.62: 'You will see the Son of man sitting at the right hand of Power, and coming with the clouds of heaven.' There would seem to me to be little doubt that this verse is dependent on the Jewish traditional interpretation of Dan. 7.13 and, in keeping with several other *parousia* references, points to an eschatological event in the unspecified future when the kingdom of God will be revealed through the appearing of 'the Son of man'.

The difficulty lies not in the evidence of such future intervention, but in its interpretation. Many attempts have been made to discredit all future reference or to explain it as a reading back of later expectation or to assert that this is simply a mistaken judgment on the part of Jesus and his disciples. All such attempts to explain away this 'contradiction' between the kingdom as a present reality and the kingdom as future event must fail, if only because at the centre of Jesus' teaching is this inherent tension which will remain unresolved until the consummation. The Baptist theologian, Eric Rust, has described the situation well in these words:

> The *eschaton*, the end of history, has already come in Jesus Christ and time has already been filled with eternity, yet the very hiddenness must end in a final consummation when the full glory shall shine forth. *Then*, what is happening in the present period of history, when the *aeons* overlap and the powers of the coming aeon are at work in historical time, will be summed up and made plain. *Then*, the judgment that is already supervening upon men and the salva-

tion that is already effective in their lives will be gathered up into a fully consummated eternal order and history will be no more. *Then*, the Christ, whose glory is known only to faith, will stand forth in his supernal splendour, and the mists of history will be taken up into the unbounded and unfettered eternity of God.[38]

It is the very disciples who, through Jesus, have entered into the kingdom and are already 'heirs of the promise' who are taught to say 'Thy kingdom come', and who pray, 'Even so, come, Lord Jesus!'

But between the coming of Jesus with the kingdom and his coming again in power lies the gift of the Spirit, with its manifest wonders and signs and the ongoing mission of the church. The exaltation of the Son of man to the right hand of God the Father is directly related to 'the mighty acts' performed by God through his church. Because 'all authority in heaven and on earth has been given' to the exalted Christ, his followers have to 'go and make disciples of all nations' (Matt. 28.18). The authority of the Son of man is demonstrated and realized through the proclamation of the Christ to all people. Berkhof points out this same connection in the parallel passage in Acts. 1.6–8 where, in reply to the question 'Lord, will you at this time restore the kingdom to Israel?', he replies, 'It is not for you to know times or seasons which the Father has fixed by his own authority. But you shall receive power when the Holy Spirit has come upon you; and you shall be my witnesses in Jerusalem and in all Judea and Samaria and to the end of the earth.'[39]

This same emphasis on the missionary task of the church as a continuation of the work of the kingdom and as a preparation for the consummation is brought out clearly in Mark 13 (with parallel passages in Matt. 24 and Luke 21) where, amidst a recounting of the signs and portents that will usher in the *eschaton*, it is clearly stated that 'the end is not yet' (v.7) and that 'the gospel must first be preached to all nations' (v.10).

There are many indications elsewhere in the teaching of Jesus, not least in some of his parables, that there will be a time of waiting after his departure from them (cf. Mark 2.19), that the kingdom will take its own time to grow (cf. Matt. 13.30), that it may not appear for some time to come (cf. Matt. 25.19) and that in the meantime the gospel is to be preached in the whole world (cf. Mark 14.9). No indication is given of the duration of the time between. What seems certain is that for Jesus, as for his followers, the kingdom that came in him and that continues through the proclamation of the gospel through his church and with the aid of his Spirit will reach its climax in his return when what is hidden will at last be revealed. As with the time of the consummation, so also with the nature of the *parousia* – it is almost entirely hidden from us. All we are told is that it is sure, that it will bring judgment and offer hope, and that it will vindicate Jesus in the eyes of the world. For the rest, it remains a mystery whose meaning and glory will one day be revealed.

4 *The transformation of apocalyptic*

We have seen, then, that apocalyptic undoubtedly contributed to the creation of that religious atmosphere in which Jesus ministered and the early church prospered and that, chiefly under the influence of Jesus himself, that atmosphere was radically changed to give a quite new climate of religious thought and expression. Or to put it another way, the Jewish apocalyptic mould in which the early church received so much of its eschatological understanding soon proved to be completely inadequate to contain or to define the gospel as it had been received from Jesus, and so the mould had to be broken and something quite different created in its place.

The apocalyptic mode of thought as a means of expressing the church's *kerygma* continued of course, as we have already observed, and is made manifest not least by the presence within the New Testament itself of writings with a marked apocalyptic identity. It is significant, however, that such writings are in fact few in number. Indeed, apart from a few fragments scattered throughout the New Testament which may be said to have an apocalyptic 'flavour', there are only three sizeable contributions: Mark 13 (with its parallels in Matt. 24 and Luke 21.5–36), Luke 17.20–37 and the book of Revelation. But in each case the differences are every bit as marked as the similarities when compared with other contemporary apocalyptic books.

In Mark 13, for example, in an otherwise apparently apocalyptic context, Jesus is said to go out of his way to decry speculation concerning the end and to deny that men are able to predict the day and the hour of its coming (cf. 13.32). Earlier in the same gospel the same point has been made. We are told that Jesus, when asked by the Pharisees for a sign from heaven, sighed deeply and said, 'Why does this generation seek a sign? Truly I say to you, no sign shall be given to this generation' (8.12). So also in the Lucan passage where Jesus tells the Pharisees quite categorically, 'The kingdom of God is not coming with signs to be observed; nor will they say "Lo, here it is!" or "There!" for behold, the kingdom of God is in the midst of you' (Luke 17.21f.).

Of greater significance in this connection is the book of Revelation. The presence of this book in the canon is a clear indication of the place given to the apocalyptic element in the *kerygma* of the early church. At the same time it is significant that this one substantial apocalyptic contribution to the New Testament was not produced until around the end of the first century and did not gain easy or early widespread recognition. In both style and content it has much in common with the earlier and contemporary Jewish apocalyptic writings and has a similar historical background of oppression and persecution. But there are some noticeable and significant differences between them. One is that, unlike its Jewish counterparts, it does not profess to be pseudonymous in authorship. The writer does not feel obliged to adopt the name of some ancient worthy to whom God revealed himself in the distant past. The device of describing past history in the form of prophecy is quite unnecessary. He, a prophet called John (1.1) on an island called Patmos, had received from God a direct revelation of Jesus Christ his living Lord, and in the light of that revelation addresses himself to specific groups of Christians throughout Asia Minor, assuring them, as a true pastor, of the grace and power of God within and beyond all their sufferings and privations. Herein lies the great difference between Revelation and the Jewish apocalyptic writings – the pivotal place it gives to the person of Jesus Christ, to his earthly historical rooting and more especially to his death upon the cross. He is portrayed not simply in apocalyptic style as a heavenly Son of man, coming from the future into the present to rout his enemies and deliver his people, but as a Lamb who was slain (5.6, 12), who was raised to life again (1.18) and is present with them now, consoling and disciplining them as they go about their mission of making known the gospel of the kingdom of God. It is as the suffering witness (*martus*) that he bears testimony to God's sovereign rule, and it is as suffering witnesses that his followers will at last share in the glories of the kingdom.

We see, then, that for all the influence of apocalyptic on the *kerygma* of the early church, that influence was limited both in volume and in content, being itself reinterpreted in the light of the person of Jesus Christ and his living presence with them. Gerhard Ebeling expresses this epigrammatically in these words: 'We do not by any means merely interpret Jesus in the light of apocalyptic, but also and above all interpret apocalyptic in the light of Jesus.'[10] This would appear to reflect faithfully the judgment of the New Testament writers and the early church as a whole.

Let me now indicate one or two specific points at which earlier apocalyptic thought was thus reinterpreted and transformed. One is to be found in the concept of history and its relation to the kingdom. According to popular apocalyptic understanding, the acts of God in history are subordinate to a predetermined pattern which develops according to an overall divine plan until it reaches its foreordained climax in the *eschaton*. Events, it would seem, are of less significance than the sequence of events; the detection of the hand of God in such events is of less importance than the identification of signs and portents and the calculation of the coming of the end and the ushering in of the age to come. As we have seen, the approach of Jesus and his followers is altogether different. It is not for his disciples 'to know times or seasons which the Father has fixed by his own authority' (Acts 1.11). The kingdom will not come as the end product of long epochs of history and as the unfolding of a detailed and determined plan at the end of time. Rather, it is the sovereign rule of God breaking into history at the point of the 'here and now' and working itself out in terms of human experience in the hearts and minds of those who will submit to that rule. Here we have a concept of history much nearer to that of the Old Testament prophets than to that of the Jewish apocalyptists. History itself is the arena of God's disclosure. Human experience is the sphere of the kingdom's operation. Human response is the means of participation in it in this present age.

This emphasis on the importance of individual response is characteristic of Jesus' teaching concerning the kingdom and introduces us to a second area of reinterpretation and transformation of current apocalyptic beliefs. The claims of the kingdom will be presented to men and women, often when they least expect it, and so they are to be on the alert, ready to respond to the revelation of God (cf. Mark 13.33ff.) – and that revelation finds its focus in none other than the person and ministry of Jesus himself. Entry into the kingdom is bound up with his eschatological offer of the forgiveness of sins to as many as repent and believe. The 'mystery' or 'secret' of the kingdom is that it is to be appropriated through faith in him and commitment to him. This is to be the message of the church's proclamation and mission. Men's hope of salvation is not to be sought beyond time and history, but in response to what they have come to know of Jesus, in whom the kingdom has come, through whom it will continue and by whom it will reach its consummation.

But (and here we come to a third area of reinterpretation) the kingdom is related not only to Jesus' person but also to his work, not only to his earthly ministry but also to his death and resurrection. This comes through clearly, as we have just seen, in the book of Revelation; but there is good reason to believe that the notion of the suffering Messiah and the relation of the cross to the kingdom can be traced right back to the consciousness and conviction of Jesus himself. Of particular interest in this connection is his understanding of the apocalyptic 'Son of man' in Daniel 7 who is to be given 'dominion and glory and kingdom' (7.14). I believe it can be convincingly argued that, in a unique way, Jesus equated the concepts of Messiah, Son of man and Suffering Servant and viewed his death and resurrection as evident signs of the kingdom's working among men. It lies beyond the scope of this lecture to establish this belief or to analyse the claim that in the mind of Jesus we find, for example, a unitive exegesis of Daniel 7 and Isaiah 53. We note that, some time before, the Covenanters of Qumran may have interpreted their mission in this way, trying by submission and endurance to effect atonement for the sin of their people after the manner of the 'Servant of the Lord'. Even if this be so the 'Son of man' and the 'Suffering Servant' remained for them societary figures. In the case of Jesus, however, the identification centres in himself and his death on the cross. When he came into Galilee preaching the 'gospel of God' (Mark 1.15), he declared that 'the time is fulfilled and the kingdom of God is at hand [cf. Dan. 2.44]: repent and believe in the gospel' (cf. Isa. 61.1ff.). The fulfilment of these ancient prophetic words he saw in himself in a way that no one else had done before. In particular, the cross was no mistake, but was part of the foreordained counsel of God. The apocalyptic Son of man was the Suffering Servant of the Lord. 'Between the coming of the Kingdom as a "mystery" and its coming "with power" ', writes A. M. Hunter, 'lies the Cross . . . The Cross was inevit-able if the "mystery" was to become an open secret. Jesus died in order that the Kingdom might come "with power"' (Mark 9.1; cf. Rom. 1.4).[41]

This emphasis is obvious also in the writings of the apostle Paul. In the epistle to the Romans, for example, the great theme of justification, for Jews and Gentiles alike, is set be-tween the pivotal points of the cross and the *eschaton*, whilst in I Corinthians the readers are to live out their lives within the tensions and travails of time and history, knowing that 'real power' is to be found only in 'weakness' and in terms of the 'word of the cross', which is nothing but a scandal to seekers after signs (cf. I Cor. 1.10ff.). This cruciform reshaping of popular apocalyptic spoke critically (and speaks critically still) to all who might be tempted to scan the heavens for signs of the kingdom's coming or to live with false notions of what that coming means.

One other point should perhaps be mentioned which indicates a further reinterpretation or transformation of popular apocalyptic. I refer to the place now given to the *kerygma* or *preached message* in heralding the kingdom over against the essentially literary character of traditional apocalyp-tic. It was hitherto believed that the divine revelations of the coming kingdom had been recorded in 'secret writings' which the apocalyptic seers must seek to interpret to 'the wise'. These supposed prophecies took the form of messages from the dis-tant past, made known through visions and auditions, whose meaning was revealed only to the *élite* among God's people. The picture in the New Testament is altogether different. Only, in a sense, by an accident of history does the tradition recorded there assume literary form. Jesus, we are told, came *preaching* the good news of the kingdom. His followers were to *preach* the gospel to every creature. His church was to *proclaim* the Lord's death till he comes. No longer were they to search the scriptures, in the manner of the apocalyptists, to find signs and portents and to record them as sealed writings for generations to come. By the power of the Holy Spirit they were to *speak* the *word* of eternal life which can become for every man and woman an immediate and personal possession.

We conclude, then, that though apocalyptic remains an expression of the *kerygma* in the New Testament, in the process of being adopted by Jesus and the early church it is transmuted and transformed. 'It is no accident', writes Ebeling again, 'that the characteristic literary form in Christianity was the gospel and not the apocalypse.'[42] Its message was not of predictions and prognostications, but of the good news of Jesus Christ, the Son of God, who lived and died and rose again, to whom had been given the power and the kingdom.

5 *Today's* kerygma

Today, as in the first century AD, the Christian church has the inescapable responsibility of proclaiming to all men the gospel of the kingdom. That means essentially 'the gospel of Jesus Christ, the Son of God' (Mark 1.1). He is the embodiment of the kingdom; through him its power is at work in the world today; and in him it will find its fulfilment in the providence and will of God. The *kerygma*, now as then, must be a proclamation of Jesus Christ who holds the key to our understanding of the kingdom at this present time and will be there at the end to give it meaning and purpose.

Such proclamation must be true to Jesus' own understanding and interpretation of the kingdom. For one thing it must avoid those prognostications and speculations which he himself decried. It must reflect too the tensions and travails that are the lot of the faithful in time and history. Above all it must acknowledge and persuade men that the crucifixion of Jesus holds the key to the mystery of the kingdom – that 'power' is to be truly known only in 'weakness' in terms of the word of the cross. This emphasis in Jesus' teaching is a corrective to the distortions which we find not only in ancient Jewish apocalyptic but also in some modern versions of it. Attempts to 'demythologize' so as to make the message relevant and enduring must always take serious account of this 'scandal' which was a stumbling-block in the first century as it is today (cf. I Cor. 1.18–24).

There are different levels at which the powers of the kingdom are seen to be at work. As we have observed, it is bound up, for example, with the individual and with the individual's response in faith to what he has seen and known of Christ. The proclamation of the kingdom is an invitation to people to commit themselves to Jesus Christ and to his way of life. The earliest disciples were known as 'followers of the way'. The way of the kingdom is the way of Jesus. To follow him is to enter the kingdom. To enter the kingdom is to profess the name of Jesus and to be his disciple. This is a present fact. But it is also a future hope which carries with it (as we shall see more fully in our next chapter) the assurance of life after death, a sharing in the resurrection of Jesus and a place in his heavenly kingdom. The New Testament is consistent throughout in its unswerving conviction that for those who believe in Jesus Christ, the Son of God, death is not the end but rather a new beginning. It is not mere survival but life in all its fullness through the resurrection of Jesus Christ from the dead. 'Because I live, you will live also' (John 14.9.). He has become 'the first-fruits of those who have fallen asleep' (I Cor. 15.20).

But the gospel is more than good news for the individual; it is good news too for present-day society in which men and women live, for all mankind and indeed for the whole created order. It is true that the kingdom is not to be identified with any one social or political system; nor is it to be welcomed in either by social emancipation or by political liberation. But we must not conclude from this that it has nothing to do with present-day society or with the hopes and fears of men and women who live under oppression or in abject poverty or in fear of nuclear obliteration. The kingdom is operative now in the world. Its unobtrusive and irresistible energies are not confined to private experience or even to the corporate life of the church. They are at work in the world, changing society, shaping history, renewing creation. The kingdom of God, says Paul, means 'righteousness, peace and joy in the Holy Spirit' (Rom. 14.17). It is surely not without significance that the word 'righteousness' comes first here and is followed immediately by the word 'peace', which in its root meaning signifies 'wholeness', 'completeness', 'harmony', 'integration'. The kingdom is about right relationships not only between men and God but also between men and men. It is about the *wholeness* of salvation when at last *all things* will be taken up into God's eternal purpose in Christ. And it is concerned about these things here and now. The church's proclamation of the kingdom is the good news of God's righteous and peaceful rule as it seeks to work itself out in this world and at this time. Its message is not abnegation of involvement in the world's affairs or a giving up of the world as lost and on the verge of destruction. Its mood is not that of pessimism and renunciation. On the contrary it is one of hope and confidence because it is *God*'s kingdom and not ours; it is the revelation of *God's* power in the affairs of men, not the working out of man's designs. For this reason its presence among us and its growth to completion are stamped with the certainty of God. The *kerygma* which saw in the passion and death of Jesus a heralding of the kingdom coming in power, cannot today lose hope even when confronted with oppression, discrimination, persecution, torture and war. The kingdom belongs to God and is at work now, overcoming the powers of evil and subduing the chaos of creation. Because this is so, today's *kerygma* must address itself to the world in which we live and to the situations in which men and women are. It is not good news in a vacuum; it is good news for particular people in particular circumstances who are crying out, corporately as well as individually, for the salvation of God.

In our first chapter we saw a relationship between the intertestamental period and our present generation, both of which are times of crisis for mankind and both of which, each in its own way, express themselves in terms of apocalyptic hope and deliverance. Indeed much secular, as well as religious, thinking today reflects the mood of apocalyptic and demonstrates the relevance of its message for this present time. That mood is peculiarly fitting to express the feelings, frustrations and hopes of our modern world, torn as it is with conflict and hopeful of the establishment of a new order of society. 'The age of the social question' has become 'the age of revolution'. Paul Lehmann, for example, talks about the recognition and assessment of violence in our day as 'an apocalyptic phenomenon' and speaks of 'a new order against an established order in and through an apocalyptic moment of truth'. The world is already lost and is 'in the act of being displaced by a new and human world already on the way'.[43] No longer, however, is it the supra-mundane world found in Jewish apocalyptic. It is the overlap of history when one era ends and a new begins. Through travail and the struggle for humanization, for such it is, the new society is born.

But here again, for the Christian, the name of Jesus is supreme. Politics and sociology are and must always be areas of Christian concern, but they must not be allowed to take the place of Jesus Christ as the content or focus of Christian preaching or Christian witness concerning the kingdom. 'The kingdom of the world', says John, 'has become the kingdom of our Lord and of his Christ' (Rev. 11.15). But that kingdom is more than the aggregate of all earthly kingdoms and its expression is more than sound politics and good government. It is inseparable from the person of Jesus Christ and its coming is bound up with the proclamation of his name.

The New Testament makes it plain that the kingdom which came with Jesus and which is even now at work in the world is yet to be revealed at the consummation when all things will be summed up in Christ (cf. Eph. 1.9ff.). The timely warnings given by Jesus in this regard were clear and to the point. It is not for us to scan the heavens for signs of the coming of the Son of man. Slide-rule theology which calculates times and seasons with allegorical arithmetic and prognosticates with precision what God has reserved for himself alone (cf. Matt. 24.36) has no place in the teaching of Jesus and should have no place in the *kerygma* of his church.

Concerning the detailed nature of the *parousia* and the time of the consummation we must profess a Christian agnosticism. But the *fact* of its coming is deeply embedded in our Lord's teaching and in the tradition of the church and must be proclaimed with the assurance of faith. The abuses to which this hope has been subjected and the excessive behaviour to which these abuses have sometimes led in the history of the church should not deter us from proclaiming with conviction the certainty of God's vindication of his Son Jesus in the eyes of the world and of his final victory when all things will be put under his feet (cf. Heb. 2.8). He who has begun a good work in Christ and continues it through his Spirit will bring it to an end and all men will see that God indeed is King. The *kerygma* is about the kingdom and the kingdom is about the Son of God.

IV

Today and Tomorrow

1 *Technology and change*

Like the apocalyptists of old there are those today who predict the end of society and of life as we have come to know it, unless certain drastic steps are taken to obviate what otherwise must be the inevitable. Not a few of them would interpret these 'drastic steps' in terms of technology and see in the process of technological change the only feasible escape-route from disaster. A timely warning against a too facile acceptance of such a solution, and indeed the dangers involved in it, is given in this comment in a recent World Council of Churches publication:

> We find ourselves at a turning point in human history. A new social order that is both just and sustainable must emerge if catastrophe is to be avoided. Time is of the essence. Some believe that it is already too late; others believe that science and technology can still find ways out. However robust, the faith of yesterday in the power of science and technology is today misplaced and therefore misleading. In fact the reductionist, triumphalist, manipulative approach of science and technology has itself been in large part responsible for our predicament.[44]

An interesting commentary on this theme is given by Alvin Toffler in his book *Future Shock*, first published in 1970. He quotes with approval the Chinese proverb, 'To prophesy is extremely difficult – especially with respect to the future', but ventures to suggest that the momentum of change will so grow during the remaining part of the twentieth century that 'an abrupt collision' with the future is inevitable. Hence the title of his book. He goes so far as to say that the magnitude of change now affecting the Western world is comparable with only one other breach in historic continuity, the shift from barbarism to civilization.

Perhaps the greatest single factor behind the accelerative thrust of change, Toffler suggests, is technology. There is a desperate need for it to be brought under control and to acquire a much greater measure of responsibility. He quotes in this connection these words of Ralph Lapp:

> We are aboard a train which is gathering speed, racing down a track on which there are an unknown number of switches leading to unknown destinations. No single scientist is in the engine cab and there may be demons at the switch. Most of society is in the caboose looking backward.[45]

If technology is not tamed and brought under control, its rush toward super-industrialism will lead to the total break-up of industrialism itself and the collapse of technocratic planning.

The time for action is well advanced; but just sufficient time is left, by careful and long-range planning, to choose a preferable future from all those alternatives which could lead to destruction. Indeed, man must take conscious control of the evolutionary process itself if he is to survive. This is the moment to anticipate the future and to design it for future survival. 'This,' he concludes, 'is the supreme instant, the turning point in history at which man either vanquishes the processes of change or vanishes.'[46]

Somewhat similar warnings are given by a Jesuit scholar, James V. Schall, in an article entitled 'Apocalypse as a Secular Enterprise'.[47] Apocalypse, he claims, has now for the first time become pre-eminently a scientific rather than a religious phenomenon so that people look not so much to theologians and preachers for future prognostications but rather to ecologists, demographers and atomic scientists (their 'doomsday clock eternally a little before midnight'). Science and technology are still regarded as the effective ameliorative factors in a world of hunger and disease, and yet 'science itself stands dangerously close to being consumed by its own self-generated prophets of doom'.

All this talk about cultural, and in particular scientific and technological, change may at first sight seem a long way from the ancient apocalyptic expectation concerning the end and its hope in the coming of the kingdom. And yet there is a close connection between them. This is seen not least in the language of crisis so often used and the apparent inevitability of the catastrophic end of society and of history as men have come to know them. It is seen, too, in the relationship between the development of modern technology (which is closely related historically to the basic Christian assumptions of Western culture) and the biblical notion of creation from which it derived its inspiration. Within technology, as within creation itself, there are felt to be destructive forces at work which have to be curbed and controlled. At the same time the promise is given of a new creation, cleansed and transformed, and as such is a reminder of the potential for good of technological achievement which may be seen as an evident sign of the kingdom's presence among men. It would be wrong, I believe, to go on from there and confuse the kingdom with some kind of technological utopia or to transpose the Christian hope concerning the end of time into trust in technological progress. But it would be equally wrong, in my opinion, to separate them in such a way as to imply that the one has nothing to do with the other. Technology may not be, as Teilhard de Chardin claimed, the springboard of man's evolution into the superhuman. We may concede, however, that there is about it an eschatological perspective of hope which God can use in working out the plan and purpose of his kingdom. Apocalyptic prophecy and scientific prediction may differ greatly, then, in content and expression, but behind

62

each is the warning of judgment and the promise of new hope.

2 Two diverse prognostications

Against this background of technological and scientific change let me now focus attention on two quite diverse prognostications which have caught the popular imagination, not least in the United States of America. Each takes seriously the dire state of the world and in particular our Western civilization. Each recognizes that this is indeed an age of crisis and impending doom. Each is apocalyptic in emphasis and content and is based on an exposition of the New Testament Apocalypse. I refer to recent writings of Hal Lindsey and William Stringfellow.

I look first at Hal Lindsey's *There's a New World Coming* (together with his earlier writings *The Late Great Planet Earth* and *Satan is Alive and Well on Planet Earth*).[48] Published in 1973, within a matter of months it had sold over one million copies. It is a fundamentalist and literalist approach to scripture which, in apocalyptic manner, interprets the book of Revelation chapter by chapter and verse by verse in terms of current events and conflicts. These indicate clearly that we are living now on the very brink of the end. The present earth will be destroyed in 'a quadrillion megaton explosion' and there will be established a new earth where Christ and his people will live in perfect peace.

With greater boldness and greater precision than any ancient apocalyptic writer, the author identifies the Soviet Union, Red China and the European Economic Community respectively in references to Gog (or 'the power from the north'), 'the king of the East' and 'the ten horns of the Beast'. Prophecies of 'fire, smoke and brimstone' are clear references to nuclear explosions, radio-active fall-out and melted earth. The locusts which appear here as agents of God's wrath are cobra helicopters; their deadly sting is the nerve gas sprayed from the helicopters' tail! The corpses of 'the two witnesses' referred to in Rev. 11 are to be seen by the people of 'all tongues and nations' – by Telstar television!

This is obviously 'popular' stuff which makes exciting reading for those who may be inclined that way. But I for one find it difficult in the extreme to give any credence whatsoever to such a literalistic and pseudo-scientific approach to scripture. Not only does it misuse scripture by using it as a wire to pick the lock of the future, it fails to take seriously the working of God within history – men and nations appear as pawns in a great game of chess in which the fate of each is determined from the beginning. It has, of course, something in common with ancient apocalyptic, but in its emphasis on prediction, its confidence in precise fulfilment and its subjective approach to prophecy it goes far beyond these ancient writers in their more extravagant moods. In particular it pays scant attention to the warnings given by Jesus, as noted in the previous chapter, against calculating times and seasons and indulging in predictions and prognostications the knowledge of which the Father has reserved for himself alone (cf. Matt. 24.36). In all these respects it discredits the tradition in which the apocalyptists stood and conveniently uses scripture to suit its own purpose.

One rather frightening by-product of this process of interpretation is that it is so easy to *create* the very situation which is being described so that the interpretation given brings about its own fulfilment. Russia, for example, is to be destroyed by nuclear attack – and scripture must be fulfilled! It needs little imagination to understand the consequences of such a belief, especially if held with deep conviction by politicians and the military who have the power to press the button and to execute the judgment thus prophesied and foreordained.

A quite different expression of modern apocalyptic is to be found in the second book to which I have referred – William Stringfellow's *An Ethic for Christians and Other Aliens in a Strange Land*. It is a reflection, against the background of

64

modern American society, on the book of Revelation and more especially on those sections within it relating to Babylon which stands under the judgment of God. The New Testament Apocalypse does not represent 'a predestinarian forecast' which is to be played out and interpreted like some 'cosmic horoscope'. To treat such biblical passages in this way as 'mechanistic prophecy' is to distort the prophetic ministry and to demean the vocation of Jesus Christ himself.

The book of Revelation, Stringfellow claims, is a political document as indeed the Bible as a whole is. It is concerned with the politics of creation and the politics of redemption, the politics of the nations and their institutions and the politics of the kingdom of God, the politics of death and the politics of life. It is about the fallenness not just of man, but also of creation itself. This means it is about the fallenness of nations, institutions, principalities and powers. All such, and not just man, share a common status as fallen creatures. They are expressions of demonic powers which are themselves agents of death. The virtues which these fallen creatures idolize – 'military prowess, material abundance, technological sophistication, imperial grandeur, high culture, racial pride' and so on – are 'ancillary and subservient to the moral presence of death' within them.

The Babylon passages are an allegory concerning death which is to be found in every nation, every corporation, every institution which, by its very nature, tends to assume the place of God and declare its autonomy over against the Almighty. The Babylon of Revelation is about the Roman empire in Domitian's reign. But it is about much more than that. It is a description of the reality that exists in each and any nation, city and institution throughout history. In particular it is archetypical of all *nations*. The spectacular example of this in the earlier part of the twentieth century was Nazi Germany. An outstanding instance at this present time, says the author (writing in 1973), is the United States of America. But death is to be found not just in the nation; it is manifest also in great ideologies like Marxism or capitalism which are so ready to pre-empt God in their demands for obedience, service and glorification. Over against Babylon, the city of death, is Jerusalem, the city of salvation. In common with every other fallen creature Babylon suffers from the delusion that she either is now, or is in process of becoming, Jerusalem. It is the delusion from which the nation, for example, suffers, when it assumes that it is sovereign and is the touchstone of moral significance for everyone else.

As such, the writer argues, the book of Revelation is in keeping with the biblical faith as a whole in proposing no other-wordly notions of the perfected society. There will indeed be a consummation of history and a transcendence of time, but Revelation relates essentially to the lives of human beings and of nations within historical circumstances. It 'contemplates no destiny for any humans or for any institutions or similar creatures beyond familiar history or outside of time'.[49]

Hope lies in coping with and in conquering death which is to be found in all earthly institutions. Such hope is focused in God's people and in the second advent of Jesus Christ. It takes shape as God's people act now in anticipation of Christ's vindication as judge of men, nations, principalities and powers. There will be no disjuncture or disruption between the second advent and the first, for the one is a consummation of the other and of those signs of the kingdom made known in Jesus' earthly ministry. The second advent assures us that death, which now prevails, is already undone and is in no way to be feared.

Thus interpreted, the 'discerning of signs' is altogether different from predestinarianism or occult prediction. It does not seek spectacular proofs or await the miraculous. It is concerned with perceiving 'the saga of salvation within the era of the Fall', seeing 'portents of death where others find progress or success' and, at the same time, recognizing 'tokens of the reality of the Resurrection or hope where others are consigned to confusion or despair'.[50]

66

I would myself question some of the conclusions to which William Stringfellow comes, not least his apparent limitation of human destiny to the confines of history and of time; but his methodology is in my judgment greatly to be preferred to that of Hal Lindsey, if only because he takes history seriously and respects the warnings of the gospels and of Jesus concerning false or presumptuous interpretations of 'the signs of the time'. By interpreting the book of Revelation in the way he does, he at the same time says something about apocalyptic itself and in particular its limitations as a vehicle of divine truth. He makes little or no use of its esoteric trappings and its highly imaginative visions of future doom and bliss, but tries to uncover its timeless message which has application and relevance in every age and not least our own. This message is essentially one of hope, born of faith in the resurrection of Jesus Christ and asserting the vindication of the people of God.

Consideration of these two prognostications, together with that of the relationship between technology and the coming kingdom, has emphasized two themes, highlighted by apocalyptic, and emerging at several points in this book (particularly in chapter II), which are well worth exploring further and about which the apocalyptists had something to say which is still of value. These are the relation – or tension – between history and the kingdom and between this life and life after death. In the last two sections of this chapter I shall consider some theological implications arising from them.

3 Continuity and discontinuity: the kingdom

I begin with the observation already made in chapter II that, in their reflections on history and the end of history, as on the kingdom present and the kingdom future, the ancient apocalyptic writers, both Jewish and Christian, thought in terms of both continuity and discontinuity.

Despite the finality and 'otherness' of the end and the coming kingdom, it is closely related to past history and to present circumstance. As we have already seen, the evil to be destroyed on the great day of judgment may take the form of demons and Satans, but these same 'principalities and powers' are to be identified now, at this present time, with oppressive princes and tyrannical rulers. The struggle against human tyranny is of one piece with 'the war to end all wars', that Armageddon in which evil will be routed and the hosts of Satan defeated.

So also with the teaching of the New Testament, and not least the teaching of Jesus. The powers of the kingdom are at work here and not just hereafter. The writer of the Apocalypse prays 'Even so, come, Lord Jesus!' (Rev. 22.20). But he can do so because that coming has in a sense already taken place: 'We give thanks to thee, Lord God almighty, who art and who wast, that thou hast taken thy great power and begun to reign' (Rev. 11.17). Christians are thus taught to regard the world, time and history not just as some kind of back-cloth against which the drama of the kingdom is performed but as the very stage on which it is lived out. The Apocalypse and the gospel apocalypses, writes J. A. T. Robinson, give us 'a Christian theology of secular history'.[51] That is, the concerns and pursuits of secular history have meaning and worth in terms of the kingdom. The contributions of technology, science, economics and politics towards the creation of a just and equitable society are not of mere incidental significance. They are, or can become, a means whereby the kingdom can become visible on earth.

But as soon as that has been said it has to be qualified, for the goal set before us is not simply a secular society hammered out by dedicated men. The kingdom cannot be confused with man-made and illusory utopias, nor will it come in the natural course of events if only we faithfully pursue a given line and adopt an agreed policy. It is true that the powers of the kingdom are already at work in history and that human beings are stewards of its mysteries and agents of its coming. But history does not move automatically or inevitably towards that goal. The kingdom which is to be understood in terms of its continuity with history must equally be understood in terms of discontinuity.

It is mundane and secular; it is also supramundane and transcendent in the sense that it is to be understood in terms and in dimensions which, though taking proper account of time and history, go far beyond them. The World Council of Churches document already quoted (p. 60 above) asserts:

> We believe that time is not infinite, that history will end, that the present heaven and earth will pass away, that the new heaven and the new earth will come, that the Kingdom of God is not something that happens in linear continuity with history. In this sense Christians are not naïve utopians or simple optimists who identify the just and sustainable society with the Kingdom of God.[52]

In apocalyptic and New Testament thought generally, the hope of the kingdom, though historically related or even historically realized, is nevertheless essentially future-orientated. Its eschatology is focused on 'the beyond'. The kingdom is something 'given'. It comes 'from above' and is the work and the gift of God. This, as we have seen, has been underlined by modern theologians like Wolfhart Pannenberg and Jürgen Moltmann. Pannenberg, for example, accepts that history is the sphere of divine revelation, but it is only at the end of history that it can be seen wholly for what it is. Moltmann's emphasis is different, but the focus is the same: it is the transcendent hope that gives meaning and purpose to the present reality.

What we have, then, is not an 'either . . . or' of 'the realized' and 'the yet-to-be', but a 'both . . . and'. On the one hand, within the historical process something is being done, being created, which contributes to and is constitutive of the kingdom. Jesus taught his disciples to pray, 'Thy kingdom come . . . *on earth*'. This earth and this time provide its *locus* and determine the pattern of its purpose. It has to do with our common humanity and is being created now out of the raw

69

material of our common life. On the other hand its coming is to be understood not just in terms of progression but also in terms of consummation, not just in terms of time but also in terms of eternity. In the total process God is at work and his kingdom is revealed.

Here, as finite creatures, we are fumbling with words, trying to express in temporal language of past, present and future, God's eternity which, in the words of Pannenberg, is 'the unity of all time': 'The truth of time is the concurrence of all events in an eternal present . . . Eternity is the unity of all time, but as such it simultaneously is something that exceeds our experience of time . . . Eternity is God's time.'[53] If this is so, we can begin to see that 'the end' is already in 'the beginning' and that in particular the beginning of the end is to be found already in the life and ministry of Jesus when he both proclaimed and demonstrated the breaking in of the kingdom. 'From now on', says Jesus, 'you will see the Son of man seated at the right hand of power, and coming on the clouds of heaven' (Matt. 26.64). His first advent is the earnest of his second advent. His death and resurrection are a demonstration of his glory (cf. John 13.31) and a sign that the kingdom has come 'with power' (cf. Mark 9.1). The kingdom will be ushered in at 'the end', but through Christ its life and citizenship are a present possession.

Away back in 1932 Dietrich Bonhoeffer preached a memorable sermon on this very theme on the text 'Thy kingdom come on earth'. Writing of his theology at that time his biographer Bethge observes: 'The two poles of Bonhoeffer's thought were . . . firmly and . . . broadly anchored – the eschatological majesty of revelation on the one hand, and the relevance of the real world on the other.'[54] This polarity, this tension, this paradox (call it what you may) is the theme of his sermon. Here are a few extracts from it.

The Church prays for the coming of God's kingdom on earth. Thy kingdom come! Yet as we pray it we are either 'otherworldly' or we are secular. To pray in either of these ways means that we no longer believe in the kingdom of God on earth . . . Otherworldliness and secularism are two sides of the same coin . . . We cannot pray for the coming of the kingdom on earth if we try to flee from the cares and responsibilities of earth . . . Neither can we pray for the kingdom with our minds full of daring utopias . . . How does the kingdom of God come to us? First, he comes himself, breaking through the law of death with the resurrection: then the earth accepts his entry into her order. The two belong together. Only when the earth accepts it can it really be broken up and entered.[55]

The kingdom is 'on earth'; the kingdom is 'from heaven'; and these two are one.

But what is to be the nature of this kingdom, this new order, this transformed society? Can we delve behind what Bultmann, for example, would regard as outworn mythologies which speak of 'a new heaven and a new earth', of 'a new creation' and of 'paradise on earth'? Identification eludes us and we are left in the land of speculation with only a few signposts to guide us. They are sufficient, however, to indicate that what is envisaged is a new world order in which will flourish a new humanity after the pattern of Christ himself. It will be a community of love prefigured, but alas not fully realized, in the church, the people of God. It is a community in which God desires that all men and indeed all creation should share. It is the community of the resurrection, as Bonhoeffer reminds us, for in the resurrection of Jesus Christ the law of death is broken and the approval of divine love is for ever made known.

And how, we may ask, will this new order, this new mode of existence come to realization? John Macquarrie in this connection makes an interesting, if speculative, suggestion. He likens it to those few 'critical leaps', as he calls them, which emerge with relative suddenness in the evolutionary process of man within 'long stretches of steady, uniform development' – like the emergence of life on earth or the emergence of personal beings. He envisages

> the emergence of a radically new type of community . . . so drastically transformed, so discontinuous with the communities we know now and so transcendent of current utopias, that it could fairly be called eschatological; and yet, as a community recognizably human, personal and fulfilling, it would be in another sense continuous with the communities we know now and already prefigured in that community we call the people of God to the extent that it is striving to manifest the new humanity of Christ.[56]

This great breakthrough will be different from all that has gone before in which the Creator with his creatures will bring to flower the hope of all the ages.

But in whatever way the kingdom is to be realized, and by whatever means, to the man or woman of faith its coming is certain and their contribution to it is clear. It is God's gift to men in Christ and at the same time a sign of their faithfulness to him. 'Thy kingdom come . . . on earth as it is in heaven.' That is how it should be, for there is little, if anything, to choose between the two.

4 *Continuity and discontinuity: life and after-life*

But this tension between 'the kingdom present' and 'the kingdom future' is not the only one to be explained in terms of continuity and discontinuity. I think also of the New Testament teaching, and within and behind that the apocalyptic teaching, concerning life and after-life and the relationship between the two. In chapter II we noted the considerable break-through made by the ancient apocalyptists in this connection and glanced at just a few of their distinctive beliefs. I want now simply to reflect briefly on the theological significance of some of these beliefs, not least as they have been shaped and refined within the Christian scriptures and the Christian tradition.

It is to the credit of the apocalyptists that they were the first, in the Hebrew–Christian tradition, clearly to point beyond this life to a life after death. This they were able to envisage in terms of resurrection. They came to believe that death is not only a break with the past, it is also a bridge to the future. The experience of death marks a lonely and decisive moment. More than any other experience it strikes a note of finality. It severs us from all that we have hitherto known. It is a conclusive break unlike any other event. This is indicated, for example, in the widely accepted Christian belief that death marks the point beyond which no human response is possible to the offer of God's grace. 'Every man is in fact living eschatologically, in the face of an end constituted by his own death', says Macquarrie.[57] It is this conviction that has given urgency so often to the proclamation of the gospel. Life is short and death is decisive.

But this is not the whole story, for death is also a bridge leading to a new order, a new dimension, a new quality of life. It is true that there is judgment, for example, in this present life and that, by faith, we may receive now God's gift of eternal life. But if death marks discontinuity, it marks also continuity; for judgment and eternal life do not cease with death. They are but the earnest of what is yet to be. There is, according to the apocalyptic and biblical tradition, a continuation of personal identity and individual consciousness beyond the grave. In many of the apocalyptic writings the moment of death, as we have seen, is decisive in relation to a man's response to divine grace. In some others, however, there is the possibility of moral change and growth, chiefly through the power of intercessory prayer. The Roman doctrine of purgatory apart, the continuity between life and after-life with its survival of consciousness implies the capability of awareness, response and decision not least on the part of those deprived of such capability during their lifetime on earth.

We note, moreover, that the form in which this belief in life

73

after death is presented is not that of the immortality of the soul, but rather that of resurrection. It is true that in many Jewish apocalyptic writings the departed are depicted in terms of discarnate souls after the manner of popular Greek thought and no doubt reflecting that belief. But it is equally true that this particular form of survival in most cases represents a temporary and transitional stage. At best these discarnate souls are but 'truncated personalities' which must await the resurrection for their true and ultimate expression. Such a conviction underlines the belief that man is a psycho-physical unity and that human personality cannot be adequately expressed in terms of soul or spirit apart from body. It emphasizes too that survival beyond death is not simply to be assumed as something automatic and inalienable to the person but is rather to be recognized as an act of God. As Oscar Cullmann puts it:

> Belief in the immortality of the soul is not belief in a revolutionary event. Immortality, in fact, is only a negative assertion: the soul does *not* die, but simply lives on. Resurrection is a *positive* assertion: the whole man, who has really died, is recalled to life by a new act of creation by God. Something has happened – a miracle of creation! For something has also happened previously, something fearful; life formed by God has been destroyed.[58]

The logic of this would seem to be that only the righteous are to be raised as the recipients of God's new creation. But from an early stage the belief arose that the wicked would also be raised – for judgment and punishment at the hands of God. Such a belief is deeply embedded in the New Testament tradition and cannot, in my opinion, be lightly dismissed.

But what is meant by 'the resurrection of the body'? In what form are the dead raised? This is a question, of course, which was a strong debating point in the early church, as Paul's letters make quite clear. And here the same tension of continuity and discontinuity appears. Is it a physical body or a transformed physical body or is it a new body altogether? There are

74

indications in the apocalyptic and biblical writings of all these possibilities corresponding to the new environment which, in the case of the righteous, is the kingdom in which they are raised to share – a physical body for an earthly kingdom and a 'spiritual' body for a transformed or heavenly kingdom. Sometimes, indeed, the impression is given that the 'spiritual body' grows *pari passu* with the physical body and that a man's righteous acts here on earth determine the fashioning of its 'replica' or heavenly counterpart (cf. Rev. 3.4; 16.15). But, as the resurrection of Jesus shows, these concepts of 'physical' and 'spiritual' are not mutually exclusive, for his resurrection body which bore the marks of crucifixion was not subject to the limitations of time or space.

The resurrection body is presented in symbolic language as 'a garment of light' or 'a garment of glory' in which the righteous man is clad. As a 'mortal man' he has died, but as a 'living personality' he remains. There is personal continuity identified in terms of 'body'; but there is also discontinuity in terms of a 'transformed' or 'new' body which is organically related not to this 'world' but to another. This 'other world' is the 'new heaven and new earth' of which I have already spoken and which itself reflects the same continuity and discontinuity which we have detected in the case of the resurrection body. John Hick expresses it thus:

> It is a 'new earth' only in the sense that it is a new situation, a different environment, another 'world'. Further, this other world is not composed of the same matter as our present earth and is not at any distance or in any direction from our sun and its planets. ... Redeemed and perfected human beings will find themselves in an ultimate situation in which God will be known as an all-pervasive presence, ... a totally God-oriented existence in an environment which expresses throughout the divine goodness.[59]

This correlation of the resurrection body with its new environment points to yet another 'tension', that between the individual and the corporate nature of ultimate salvation. John Robinson writes:

> The resurrection of the body, like Christianity itself, is something social; it is 'put on' as we are brought into Christ and built up into his body. That is why the resurrection of the body is always associated in the New Testament with the *Totus Christus*, the Complete Man, the revelation of Jesus Christ with all his saints.[60]

'In the mystical body of Christ', says Hick, 'humanity is to become one in many and many in one.'[61] Thus the synthesis of the eschatologies of the community and of the individual, which Ezekiel for example attempted unsuccessfully within the sphere of this present life, is at last brought about. 'The perfected individual will have become a personality without egoity, a living consciousness which is transparent to the other consciousnesses in relation to which it lives in a full community of love.'[62] The community of the resurrection (for such it is) will be seen to be 'no longer self-enclosed egos but members of a perfect community of mutually open centres of consciousness' which will express itself in 'the interpersonality of mutual love'.[63] This is that *agapē* which is shown forth supremely in the life and teaching of Jesus Christ, is the mark of his church and is the earnest of a new humanity to be made one in him.

NOTES

Chapter I   An Age of Crisis (pp. 1–20)

1. H. H. Rowley, *The Relevance of Apocalyptic*, 1944, 3rd edn. revised, Lutterworth Press 1963, Association Press 1964.

2. James Barr, 'Jewish Apocalyptic in Recent Scholarly Study', *Bulletin of the John Rylands Library* 58.1, Manchester, Autumn 1975, p. 33.

3. E. Käsemann, 'The Beginnings of Christian Theology', *New Testament Questions of Today*, Eng. trs. SCM Press and Fortress Press 1969, pp. 82–107.

4. W. Pannenberg, 'Redemptive Event and History', *Basic Questions in Theology*, Eng. trs. SCM Press and Fortress Press 1970, pp. 15–80.

5. K. Koch, *The Rediscovery of Apocalyptic*, Eng. trs. SCM Press and Allenson 1972, pp. 112ff.

6. S. B. Frost, *Old Testament Apocalyptic*, Epworth Press 1952, p. 76.

7. Hymns of Thanksgiving III, 7–10, *The Dead Sea Scrolls in English*, trs. G. Vermes, 2nd edn., Penguin Books 1975, p. 157.

8. Herbert Butterfield, *Christianity and History*, G. Bell and Scribner's 1949, p. 60.

9. Karl Barth, *Church and State*, Eng. trs. of *Rechtfertigung und Recht*, SCM Press and Macmillan, Toronto, 1939, p. 77.

10. R. Niebuhr, *Do the State and Nation Belong to God or the Devil?*, SCM Press 1937, p. 10.

11. A. Toynbee, *An Historian's Approach to Religion*, Oxford University Press 1956, p. 46.

Chapter II   From Creation to Consummation (pp. 21–40)

12. Koch, op. cit., p. 33.

13. Ibid., pp. 28ff.

14. Harvey Cox, *On Not Leaving It To The Snake*, SCM Press and Macmillan, New York, 1968, pp. 38f.

15. R. Travers Herford, *Talmud and Apocrypha*, Soncino Press 1933, p. 268.

16. G. F. Moore, *Judaism in the First Centuries of the Christian Era*, vol. I, Harvard University Press 1927, p. 127.

17. W. Lüthi, *The Church to Come*, Eng. trs. Hodder & Stoughton and Musson, Toronto, 1939, p. x.

18. E. Käsemann, 'The Beginnings of Christian Theology', *New Testament Questions of Today*, p. 102.

19. G. Caird, 'Eschatology and Politics', *Biblical Studies in Honour of William Barclay*, Collins and Westminster Press 1976, pp. 84f.

20. H. Berkhof, *Christ the Meaning of History*, Eng. trs. SCM Press and John Knox Press 1966, p. 180.

21. Harvey Cox, op. cit., pp. 38f.

22. G. Gutierrez, *A Theology of Liberation*, Orbis Books 1973, SCM Press 1974, pp. 214f., 218.

23. E. R. Bevan, *Jerusalem under the High-Priests*, Edward Arnold and Longmans, New York, 1904, p. 86.

24. W. Pannenberg, 'Dogmatic Theses on the Doctrine of Revelation', *Revelation as History*, Eng. trs. Macmillan, New York, 1968, Sheed & Ward 1969, p. 131.

25. Gutierrez, op. cit., p. 213.

26. J. Moltmann, *Theology of Hope*, Eng. trs. SCM Press and Harper & Row 1967, pp. 137f.

27. O. E. Costas, *The Church and its Mission*, Tyndale House, Wheaton, Ill., 1974, p. 261.

28. E. Jacob, *Theology of the Old Testament*, Eng. trs. Hodder & Stoughton and Harper Bros. 1958, p. 196.

29. Sigmund Mowinckel, *He that Cometh*, Eng. trs. Blackwell and Abingdon Press 1956, p. 271.

30. Moltmann, op. cit., pp. 20f.

31. A. Dumas, 'The Christian's Secular Hope and his Ultimate Hope', in *Technology and Social Justice*, ed. R. H. Preston, SCM Press and Judson Press 1971, p. 183.

32. The Book of Mysteries, *The Dead Sea Scrolls in English*, pp. 209f.

33. H. H. Rowley, *The Relevance of Apocalyptic*, 3rd edn., p. 177.

34. Cf. D. S. Russell, *The Method and Message of Jewish Apocalyptic*, SCM Press and Westminster Press 1964, ch. xiv.

Chapter III   Kingdom and Kerygma *(pp. 41–59)*

35. H. Berkhof, *Christ the Meaning of History*, p. 55.

36. Ernest Best, *The Temptation and the Passion*, Cambridge University Press 1965, p. 15.

37. C. H. Dodd, *The Apostolic Preaching and its Developments*, 2nd edn., Hodder & Stoughton 1944 (= *The Apostolic Preaching*, Harper Bros. 1950), p. 47.

38. Eric C. Rust, 'Time and Eternity in Biblical Thought', *Theology Today* 10, Princeton October 1953, p. 349.

39. Berkhof, op. cit., p. 70.

40. G. Ebeling, 'The Beginnings of Christian Theology', in *Apocalypticism*, ed. R. W. Funk, *Journal for Theology and the Church* 6, New York 1969, p. 58.

41. A. M. Hunter, *Introducing New Testament Theology*, SCM Press and Westminster Press 1957, p. 45.

42. Ebeling, op. cit., p. 53.

43. P. Lehmann, *The Transfiguration of Politics*, Harper & Row and SCM Press 1975, p. 262.

Chapter IV   Today and Tomorrow (pp. 60–76)

44. 'The Contribution of Faith, Science and Technology in the Struggle for a Just and Sustainable Society', *Anticipation* 23, World Council of Churches, Geneva, November 1976, p. 29.

45. A. Toffler, *Future Shock*, Random House and Bodley Head 1970, p. 431.

46. Ibid., pp. 485f.

47. J. V. Schall, 'Apocalypse as a Secular Enterprise', *Scottish Journal of Theology* 29.4, Edinburgh 1976, pp. 357–73; quotations from pp. 357, 359.

48. Hal Lindsey, *There's a New World Coming*, Harvest House, Irvine, California, 1973, Coverdale House 1974; *The Late Great Planet Earth*, Zondervan, Grand Rapids, Michigan, 1970; *Satan is Alive and Well on Planet Earth*, Zondervan 1972, Marshall, Morgan & Scott 1973.

49. W. Stringfellow, *An Ethic for Christians and Other Aliens in a Strange Land*, Word Books, Waco, Texas, 1973, p. 36.

50. Ibid., p. 139.

51. J. A. T. Robinson, *On Being the Church in the World*, SCM Press and Abingdon Press 1960, p. 156 n. 1.

52. *Anticipation* 23, November 1976, p. 29.

53. W. Pannenberg, *What is Man?*, Fortress Press 1970, p. 74.

54. E. Bethge, *Dietrich Bonhoeffer*, Collins and Harper & Row 1970, pp. 189f.

55. Dietrich Bonhoeffer, 'Thy Kingdom Come on Earth', Eng. trs., *The Expository Times* 88.5, Edinburgh, February 1977, pp. 146ff.

56. J. Macquarrie, *The Faith of the People of God*, SCM Press and Scribner's 1972, p. 108.

57. Ibid., p. 105

58. O. Cullmann, *Immortality of the Soul or Resurrection of the Dead?*, Epworth Press and Macmillan, New York, 1958, p. 27.

59. John Hick, *Death and Eternal Life*, Collins 1976, Harper & Row 1977, p. 189.

60. J. A. T. Robinson, op. cit., p. 132.

61. Hick, op. cit., p. 462.

62. Ibid., p. 460.

63. Ibid., pp. 462f.

INDEXES

INDEX OF SUBJECTS

Culture (*cont.*)
  conformation to, 9 ff.
  Greek, 7

Dead Sea Scrolls, 2, 9, 19f., 36, 53
Dea Roma, 14
Demons, 1, 22, 36ff., 42, 45, 65, 68
Demythologizing, 1, 37, 56, 71
Deportation, 15
Dispersion, 2, 9, 25
Divus Caesar, 14
Domitian, 65
Dreams, 1
Dualism, 24, 34

Eastern Europe, 11
End
  corresponds to beginning, 34f., 70
  evil destroyed at, 36
  nearness of, 63
  relation to history, 22, 24ff., 28ff., 32f., 46, 47, 51f., 67f.
  signs of, 36, 48, 50
  speculation on, 22, 50, 55, 64
Eschatology
  and apocalyptic, 31, 35
  and cosmology, 34f.
  and 'new society', 27
  synthesis of, 76
  tension within, 34
Eschaton (*see* End)
Eusebius, 7
Evil
  cosmic, 36ff.
  in creation, 34
  origin of, 35f.
  powers of, 35ff.
Evil spirits (*see* Demons)
Existentialism, 31
Exorcism, 37, 42, 45
Ezekiel, 39, 76

Fascism, 17

Gentiles, 40, 54
Germany, 13, 65
Gog, 63
Greek
  cities, 7, 9

  language, 9
  names, 10
Gurus, 8

Hasidim, 10, 19
Hasmoneans, 18, 27
Hell, 39
Hellenism, 7, 9, 16
Helsinki, 17
Herod, 27
History
  and contemporaneity, 24ff.
  and divine purpose, 28ff.
  and end, 22, 24ff., 28., 32f., 46, 47, 51f., 67f.
  and kingdom, 24ff., 28ff., 51ff.
  moral factor in 13
  understanding of, 21
  unity of, 32f.
Hitler, 23
Hope, theology of, 24, 31f., 69
Human rights, 15ff., 24

Immortality, 74
Individual, 27, 34, 39, 52, 56, 73, 76

Jesus
  and *agape*, 76
  and exorcism, 42, 45
  and kingdom, 41, 43f., 46ff., 50, 52f., 55ff., 68
  and messianic secret, 42f.
  and Son of man, 43, 46, 48, 51, 53, 70
  and speculation, 50, 55, 64
  death of, 45, 51, 53f.
  parousia of, 43, 46, 47, 49, 59, 70
  pre-eminence of, 3f.
  re-interpretation by, 50ff.
  resurrection of, 44, 45, 46, 53, 67, 71
  revelation of, 51
Jewish War, 3
John the Baptist, 40
Josephus, 7
Judgment
  and day of Lord, 39f., 46
  as crisis, 12
  day of, 26, 49, 68, 73
  inevitability of, 13

82

Spirit
  and coming kingdom, 48
  Holy, 48, 55, 57
State, 12ff., 17, 26
Synagogue, 26
Syncretism, 8

Technology, 60ff., 67, 68
Temple, 16
Tiberius, 5, 15

Time
  and eternity, 70
  biblical, 35
  two ages, 25

Violence, 18ff., 24, 58

Zealots, 25f.
Zeus, 12, 16
Zoroaster, 7

INDEX OF AUTHORS

INDEX OF TEXTS